Prior Learning Assessment:

A Guidebook to
American Institutional Practices

Brian J. Zucker

Chantell C. Johnson

Thomas A. Flint

CAEL

THE COUNCIL FOR ADULT & EXPERIENTIAL LEARNING

Chicago

KENDALL/HUNT PUBLISHING COMPANY
4050 Westmark Drive   Dubuque, Iowa 52002

© 1999 by the Council for Adult & Experiential Learning

ISBN 0-7872-5589-0

Printed in the United States of America
10 9 8 7 6 5 4 3 2 1

 56

Acknowledgments

Many organizations and individuals contributed to the making of this study. The study would not have been possible without a grant from the W.K. Kellogg Foundation of Battle Creek, Michigan, which provided funding beginning in 1994 in connection with the project For a Nation of Lifelong Learners (NLL). The Kellogg grant culminated in the Creating a Nation of Lifelong Learners Conference in November, 1997, in Washington, DC. Nearly 700 representatives from higher education, business, labor, policy, and philanthropy gathered to explore the many facets of adult education at this conference, jointly founded by the American Council on Education (ACE), Regents College, Empire State College and the Council for Adult and Experiential Learning (CAEL).

Principal investigator for the Prior Learning Assessment (PLA) Survey was Dr. William Maehl of Maehl Associates. Assisting Dr. Maehl was a committee from NLL founding institutions, including: Dr. Jane Altes, Empire State College; Dr. Paula Peinovich, Regents College; Dr. Steven Nunes, CAEL. As work progressed on this study, portions of the work were subcontracted to the Evaluation Consortium at the State University of New York at Albany. In addition, survey validation was conducted by a panel of experts that included Dr. Joan Knapp of Knapp & Associates, Dr. William Husson of Regis University, and Dr. Robert McMorris. A pilot version of the survey was conducted by Dr. Harriet Cabell of the University of Alabama at Tuscaloosa, Dr. Duane Anderson of East Central University in Oklahoma, Dr. Catherine Marienau of DePaul University in Illinois, and Dr. Diana McGary of Capital University in Ohio. CAEL's former Director of Institutional Relations Helen McBride assisted in contacting many institutions in order to maximize the return rate of this PLA survey.

In late 1997 CAEL's newly-appointed Vice President for Lifelong Learning Dr. Thomas Flint engaged the services of the Human Capital Research Corporation (HCRC) to assure the integrity of data capture from the survey and to produce the analysis which follows. While the Evaluation Consortium produced a trio of technical reports focusing upon survey methodology and extensive data coding structures, the material within this report deals with substantive and contextual matters of interest to PLA practitioners.

HCRC President Brian Zucker and analyst Chantell Johnson, in cooperation with Tom Flint and Ruth Chapman of CAEL, designed the analysis for reporting these findings. (Ruth Chapman and Mary Fugate wrote the previous CAEL report on PLA institutional practices published in 1992). The authors of this report express their appreciation to CAEL for the funding support during the 1997–98 fiscal year, enabling data recapture, analysis, reporting, and now, publication.

Brian Zucker, Chantell Johnson—Human Capital Research Corporation
Thomas Flint—Council for Adult and Experiential Learning

September, 1998
Chicago, Illinois

Contents

List of Figures and Tables

Chapter 1
Background

Current institutional practices in Prior Learning Assessment (PLA) may be considered to have roots in two American phenomena: the creation of regional institutional accrediting agencies to assure standards of educational quality in curricula at both the secondary and postsecondary level, and the development of methods of individual assessment stemming from the work of Sir Francis Galton but burgeoning early this century in the standardized testing movement.

By establishing curricular standards, accrediting agencies laid the foundation for comparability between institutions at the same educational level, and for distinguishing college-level learning from that which must precede it. As a consequence, as student learners became mobile, traveling between institutions before the completion of their degrees, social pressure would naturally occur for recognition (rather than repetition) of equivalent coursework satisfactorily completed at the prior institution. Simultaneously, coursework completed at the secondary level could be similarly identified, equated, and thereby denied applicability toward college degree requirements.

Just as the differences between levels of educational institutions came to be identified and standardized, so too has the identification of individual differences become more and more refined. Recognition of differences in individual capability has led in the schools to the establishment of standardized tests of educational achievement, having a two-fold effect. First, the evaluation of classroom learning came to be separated from individual teacher assessments. By implication, then, educators could come to believe that learning could be evaluated independently of the source of that learning (which in the case of the classroom has been assumed to be the instructor). Second, to the extent that some students within secondary schools performed at consistently high levels on standardized tests, educators came to believe that such students could (or would) perform at levels equal to college students. In response, testing programs such as Advanced Placement were established more than 30 years ago; high schools began to offer preparatory curricula on subject matter specialties measured by Advanced Placement tests and colleges began to award college credit for satisfactory test performance, with or without the student having taken preparatory studies.

Thus, methods of Prior Learning Assessment (PLA) rest upon the notions that creditable college-level learning is both measurable and independent of its source. The original CAEL founded in 1974 was a project housed within the Educational Testing Service and was known as the Cooperative Assessment of Experiential Learning. This project investigated and eventually validated a variety of assessment techniques for measuring college-level learning acquired experientially—that is, without formal instruction. The story of CAEL's history is told in Zelda Gamson's 1989 book, *Higher Education and the Real World*.

At least two other developments have occurred as the implications of PLA methods have been realized. First, much experiential learning occurs outside a classroom, though some of it occurs in classrooms that are outside the formal, traditional educational system. Specifically, the military and many businesses conduct educational programs for their own purposes for those they employ. Consequently, applying the concepts that college-level learning is both measurable and independent of its source, the completion of formal educational programs at unaccredited organizations may nonetheless be recognized by many colleges and universities. Though some institutions do their own assessments of the educational content from these providers, this process has also been facilitated by programs and guidelines of the American Council on Education (described below).

Second, as business and commerce has increasingly become a global phenomena, multinational companies wishing to establish human resource systems dealing equitably with educational achievement as a factor in employee job qualifications, promotions, and transfers, have begun attempts to equate learning and coursework across national boundaries. In response, educational institutions have begun to act through professional associations to articulate standards and equivalencies for educational achievement worldwide. In all these instances, methods of Prior Learning Assessment have informed both the policies and practices within these organizations.

At the same time as PLA methodologies have evolved and PLA applications have expanded, the number of "non-traditional" aged students has increased dramatically. Buoyed by the changing demands of the workforce, stagnant earnings for those with no postsecondary education along with greater eligibility for loans and other forms of financial aid, and an expansion in evening classes, weekend colleges, daycare services and other accommodations, the proportion of adults seeking a college degree has increased nearly fourfold since the 1960's. Bringing a wealth of lifetime experiences acquired through employment, raising families, military and public service, older students have been a driver of PLA and a transformative influence on the organization and delivery of postsecondary education.

Whether it is from an institutional, student or employer perspective, the formal practice of PLA has served to foster greater linkages between the classroom, other learning environments and the practical needs of society. In turn these linkages have served to strengthen the social and economic contributions of postsecondary education and foster greater opportunity. Even as the nation's baby boomer cohort moves into their 40's and 50's (and presumably towards endeavors other than a college degree), their numbers and presence (in defiance of most enrollment forecasts) on college campuses continue to grow and along with it the role and significance of PLA. Coupled with a rise in alternative postsecondary learning experiences and resources such as corporate training, Web and media-based education, the expansion and refinement of PLA by an ever increasing number of accredited providers is almost destined to continue.

INTRODUCTION

The Council for Adult and Experiential Learning (CAEL) has worked since 1974 with accrediting bodies, employers, and education organizations to develop a common language and foundation for assessing prior learning. CAEL has published a wide array of information including: standards of quality assurance; guidelines for implementing portfolio PLA by subject matter or discipline and by institutional educational approaches; sample portfolios; and, institutional PLA research. In addition, CAEL has held many events annually to disseminate information related to prior learning, developed networks among institutions interested in prior learning, and trained administrators and faculty in the procedures of prior learning assessment.

As part of this ongoing effort, CAEL has conducted several major surveys to gather detailed information regarding institutions' recognition of prior learning as well as their policies and procedures for assessment. The most recent surveys were conducted in 1991 and 1996. Each survey project invited accredited post-secondary institutions to participate (a total of 3,694 in 1991 and approximately 2,421 in 1996).[1] Information collected through these surveys has been and will be used to develop CAEL's programs and services, and to improve its capacity to further the prior learning assessment (PLA) movement.

The following report summarizes the findings of the 1996 CAEL Survey of Prior Learning Assessment (PLA). A total of 1,135 out of a total of 2,421 institutions responded to the survey (60 percent private and 40 percent public)—for an overall response rate of 47 percent (*See Appendix A for details*).

WHAT IS PRIOR LEARNING ASSESSMENT?

There are, perhaps, as many ways to define and assess PLA as there are institutions. Generally, PLA refers to any knowledge-building or skills-attainment that occurs prior to enrollment or outside of enrollment at a post-secondary institution, assessed for the purpose of awarding college credit. The history of PLA dates back as early as World War II when the American Council on Education began assessing knowledge and skills gained in the military. This initial assessment was followed by formalized testing in the mid-sixties and the assessment movement led by CAEL beginning in the mid-seventies.[2]

The term "prior learning" has evolved to encompass the knowledge and skills one attains as a result of life experiences, including volunteer service, travel, parenting and employment experiences as well as non-credit courses and independent studies. The policies to assess and award college credit for such experiences vary widely by institution. To date, nine distinct accrediting processes and procedures have been adopted by colleges and universities and are used in varying degrees as the primary tools of PLA. These procedures can be categorized into four types of PLA: standardized exams, challenge exams, guidelines for assessment, and individual assessment.

Standardized Exams

Advanced Placement Examinations (AP): AP exams are typically offered to high school students who have completed an AP course in high school and are seeking credit at the college level. Credits from the exam tend to correspond with the length of the course—3 credits per semester.

College Level Examination Program (CLEP): CLEP exams have been developed to test and assess knowledge and skills gained through non-collegiate experiences. CLEP exams include both a general test and a subject specific exam. The general exam is broad and covers several subjects—similar to what is learned in the first two years of college, while the subject specific exam includes materials covered in a specific course offered at a particular college.

American College Testing Proficiency Examination Program (ACT/PEP): ACT has developed subject specific tests for the assessment of students' knowledge and skills. These tests reflect knowledge and skills that could have been gained in a one or two semester course. Most of the exams are multiple choice, while a few require written essays. A total of 42 different courses are covered by these exams.

Defense Activity for Non-Traditional Support (DANTES): DANTES has created certification examinations that may be used to assess competency and achievement in a particular area. These exams are targeted, in part, toward military personnel; however, anyone is eligible to take any one of the 30 exams offered.

---

[1] The project was guided by a steering committee composed of representatives from Regents College, State University of New York, Empire State College (SUNY), the Council on Adult and Experiential Learning (CAEL), the American Council on Education (ACE), and Maehl Associates.

[2] Lamdin, Lois. (1997) *Earn College Credit For What You Know* (3rd Edition). Dubuque, Iowa: Kendall/Hunt Publishing Company.

Challenge Exams

Institution Based Exams (Departmental or Course Challenge Exams): Individual colleges and universities may develop, based upon the requirements and demands of their unique curriculum, exams to test students' knowledge and skills compared to the college's course requirements. Often these are the same tests used as final exams in the specified courses.

Guidelines for Assessment

American Council on Education Program on Non-collegiate Sponsored Instruction (ACE PONSI/CREDIT): ACE publishes recommendations for credit awarded for non-collegiate sponsored programs and creates exams that may be used to test or assess a student's knowledge and skill level after program completion.

American Council on Education Recommendations on Military Training (ACE/Military): Similar to the ACE PONSI/CREDIT recommendations, ACE has created measures for assessing technical skills such as those gained through military training or other technical, vocational or occupation specific knowledge and skills.

Individual Assessment

Institution-based assessment through portfolio review or oral interview: Individual colleges and universities have developed processes for assessing students' life and work experiences through an examination of these specific experiences.

Assessment of nationally recognized certificates of achievement: Individual colleges and universities may accept certificates of achievement awarded by nationally recognized organizations for such work-related experience as that obtained through the achievement of a real estate agent license or a journeyman's card.

These various types of prior learning assessment vary according to several distinct aspects of their design including, but not limited to: 1) the methodology employed (quantitative versus qualitative) for measurement; 2) the level of effort required by the learner and the institution; 3) the environment in which the knowledge, skills and abilities are demonstrated (academic test-based versus an applied learning demonstration); and, 4) whether the credit award recommendations are primarily externally derived (at the national level) or internally derived (through the faculty at the institution).

PURPOSE OF THE STUDY

The 1996 CAEL Survey of Prior Learning Assessment (PLA) was designed to serve multiple purposes. Among CAEL's goals are the following:

Develop a comprehensive PLA database: CAEL is committed to creating and maintaining a nationwide database of detailed information regarding college and university policies and use of PLA. This database may be readily combined with other public data sources to provide a more comprehensive understanding of what types of institutions offer PLA and how.

Build awareness about and facilitate the use of PLA: From this database, CAEL will be able to publish information regarding practices for assessing prior learning across a range of colleges and universities. Such information will be used in CAEL's future publications, newsletters and conferences to inform and build awareness among both institutions and adult learners.

Building a database and awareness among both post-secondary institutions and adult learners is focused toward increasing institutions' recognition of PLA and advancing its use.

Improve CAEL's programs and services and refine CAEL's strategic plan: The information will be used to frame CAEL's publications, to target conference invitations and to inform aspects of CAEL's program planning efforts.

With these three goals in mind, the PLA survey explored the following research questions:

◆ **Who is offering PLA?** This line of exploration examines the patterns of PLA use according to institutional type (public, private, urban, rural, associate's degree granting or above, etc.) and explores the type of student served by these institutions.

◆ **What methods are used to assess prior learning?** This line of exploration examines the types of systems that institutions have established to assess prior learning—addressing such questions as: What are these systems and how do they differ? Are some models or systems more commonly used or more easily implemented than others?

◆ **How has PLA changed over time?** Examining PLA over time may provide insight into the nature, status and future of PLA use among various colleges and universities. Specifically, the survey explores existing and emerging PLA trends and the implications of these trends.

◆ **What are the best practices of PLA administration?** The survey explores PLA use for any patterns, institutional policies or structures that facilitate, enhance or improve the use of PLA.

◆ **What challenges to administering PLA are apparent?** The survey explores the perceived and real challenges to the use of PLA.

SURVEY METHODOLOGY

In conjunction with a steering committee of colleges, universities and higher education representatives, CAEL developed the 1996 Prior Learning Assessment Survey (*See Appendix A*). The survey questionnaire was mailed first to a pool of post-secondary institutions accredited by agencies recognized by the Council on Post-secondary Accreditation (COPA) that were believed to have prior learning—overall a total of approximately 2,421 questionnaires were mailed. The survey cover letter was addressed to both the president and the registrar and included instruction that the most appropriate person should respond. Four weeks after the initial mailing, a follow-up or reminder post card was mailed.

Chapter 2
Profile of Responding Institutions

The 1996 CAEL Prior Learning Assessment Study resulted in completed surveys from 1,135 accredited institutions. The overall response rate to the 1996 survey was 47 percent—similar to the response rate achieved in 1991.

Data presented on the following pages compares the distribution of survey respondents for the 1996 survey with the universe of accredited colleges and universities as reported by IPEDS. While the profile of the 1991 survey population is referenced, data for this population is not shown in any of the following tables and charts.

In broad terms, the 1996 survey respondent population is similar in profile to the universe of accredited colleges and universities across a range of characteristics—with one notable distinction—survey respondents include greater representation of independent liberal arts colleges and comprehensive universities.

This difference in profile results in the following: a slightly greater representation of private versus public institutions; a comparatively greater representation of four-year versus two-year institutions; a disproportionate number of colleges and universities from the North Central and Middle state regions and under representation from the Southern and Western parts of the country; and, a greater proportion of mid-sized institutions (headcount enrollment of 1,001 to 5,000 students).

Because the original sample file was unavailable for this analysis, it is not known whether these differences in representation are the result of a respondent bias or a sampling bias or both. In addition without information regarding the construction of the original sample, it is not possible to assign sampling probability weights that would reflect the universe of potential respondents. Finally, because it is unknown whether non-respondent institutions maintain similar PLA practices as their survey counterparts, observations drawn from this study are not intended to serve as inferences about the behaviors of all accredited colleges and universities.

These caveats notwithstanding, the 1996 survey results reported herein profiles the characteristics and practices of prior learning assessment for 1,135 institutions dispersed across a range of characteristics.[3]

---

[3] For the sample to be statistically representative requires an analysis of the original population invited to participate in the survey. As a result of limitations at the time of this publication such an analysis is not possible. As a surrogate to such a statistically precise analysis, the 1996 sample data was explored according to six institutional characteristics, including control (public versus private), Carnegie Classification, region, urbanization, size, and percent minority students and was compared to the 1995–1996 Integrated Postsecondary Education Data Set of regionally accredited institutions. Based upon these comparisons, the 1996 CAEL data set may be said to be somewhat representative of the population as a whole.

General Characteristics

The sample of respondents from the 1996 survey differed from the 1991 sample with a greater percentage of private institutions responding than public. In addition, the 1996 sample differed slightly from the population of accredited institutions, where a balance exists between the number of public and private institutions.

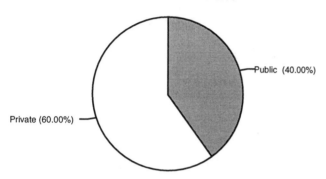

Institutional Status of Respondents
Public versus Private

Public (40.00%)
Private (60.00%)

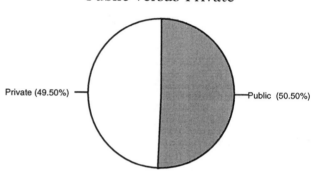

Population of Accredited Institutions
Public versus Private

Private (49.50%)
Public (50.50%)

Nearly three-fourths of the responding institutions are from master's, bachelor's and associate's degree institutions with fewer from research or doctoral institutions. In 1991, the sample of respondents represented a similar proportional breakdown across Carnegie Classifications (*See Appendix A for definition of the Carnegie Classifications*).[4]

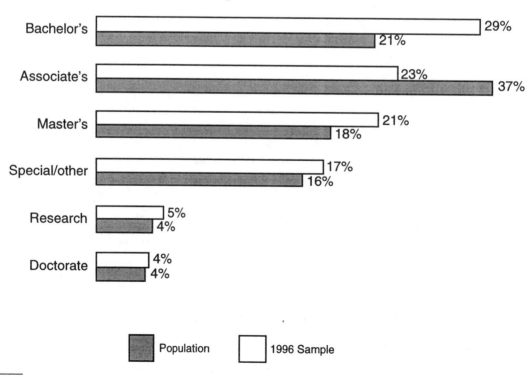

Carnegie Classification

Bachelor's — 29% / 21%
Associate's — 23% / 37%
Master's — 21% / 18%
Special/other — 17% / 16%
Research — 5% / 4%
Doctorate — 4% / 4%

Population   1996 Sample

[4] Note: the Carnegie Classification marks the highest degree conferred from an institution, not the *only* level of degree conferred.

Institutions participating in the survey come from all regions across the country, similar to the nation-wide distribution of institutions. In comparing the 1996 respondents to the 1991 respondents, the regional distribution across census regions is similar. The only exception is that the 1996 survey yielded a slightly higher response rate from the New England and Mid-Atlantic states than the 1991 survey *(See Appendix A)*.

Census Region Classification

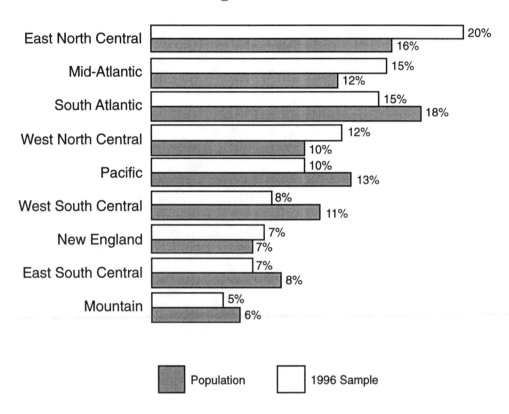

| | Population | | 1996 Sample |

Institutions were also compared according to their accrediting agency region *(See Appendix A)*. The sample of respondents appears to be somewhat proportional to the population of accredited institutions according to regional accrediting agency classification.

Institutions were also examined for their more specific location within an urban or rural area.[5] The distribution of the 1996 responding institutions generally matches the national distribution.

---

[5] **Large City**: A central city of a CMSA or MSA with the city having a population greater than or equal to 250,000. **Mid-size City**: A central city of a CMSA or MSA, with the city having a population less than 250,000. **Urban Fringe of Large City**: Any incorporated place, CDP, or non-place territory within a CMSA or MSA of a Large City and defined as urban by the Census Bureau. **Urban Fringe of Mid-size city**: Any incorporated place, CDP, or non-place territory within a CMSA or MSA of a Large city or a Mid-size City and defined as urban by the Census Bureau. **Large Town**: An incorporated place or CDP with a population greater than or equal to 25,000 and located outside a CMSA or MSA. **Small Town**: An incorporated place or CDP with a population less than 25,000 and greater than or equal to 2,500 and located outside a CMSA or MSA. **Rural**: Any incorporated place, CDP, or non-place territory designated as rural by the Census Bureau. **NA**: not assigned.

Accrediting Region Classification

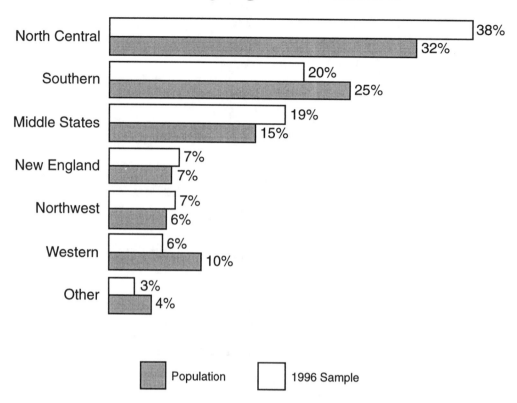

	Population	1996 Sample
North Central	32%	38%
Southern	25%	20%
Middle States	15%	19%
New England	7%	7%
Northwest	6%	7%
Western	10%	6%
Other	4%	3%

☐ Population ☐ 1996 Sample

Degree of Urbanization

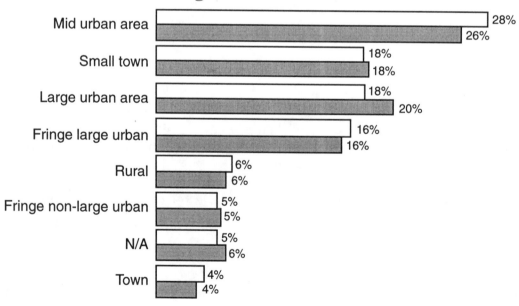

	Population	1996 Sample
Mid urban area	26%	28%
Small town	18%	18%
Large urban area	20%	18%
Fringe large urban	16%	16%
Rural	6%	6%
Fringe non-large urban	5%	5%
N/A	6%	5%
Town	4%	4%

☐ Population ☐ 1996 Sample

Enrollment Characteristics

Nearly half of the respondents are mid-size institutions. Compared to all accredited institutions nationwide, the 1996 data represents a slight overrepresentation of mid-size institutions and a slight underrepresentation of small institutions.

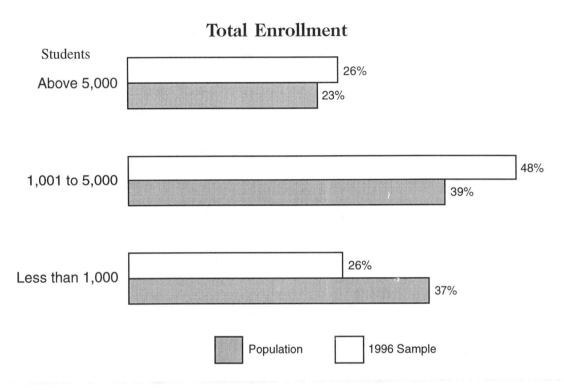

The majority of the institutions in the sample enroll a smaller percentage of minority students than the national average of 20 percent (for the academic year 1990–1991).[6]

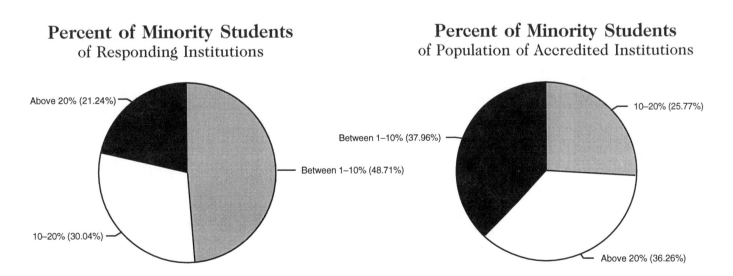

---

[6] State Higher Education Profiles. NCES (1991–1992). Table 14. Percentage distributions of undergraduate enrollment and population (ages 18–24) and undergraduate enrollment as a percentage of population (ages 18–24), by race-ethnicity and by control and level of institution.

Non-traditional students were defined in this analysis as those students at the undergraduate level who are 25 years and older. According to the comparisons presented in the following chart, the population of institutions has a greater proportion of institutions represented in the "low" percentage of non-traditional students category (with a student population of between 0–7 percent non-traditional students).

Percent of Non-Traditional Students

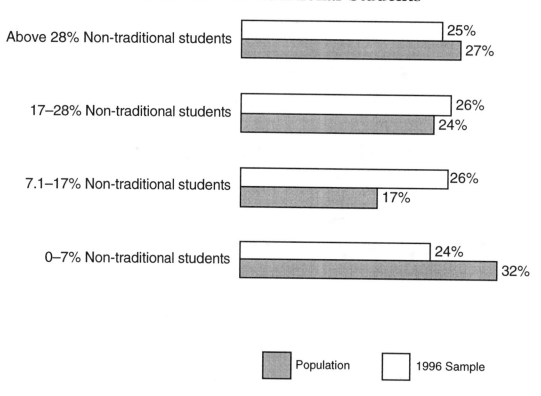

Chapter 3
Profile of PLA Users: Who Offers PLA?

O ver 84 percent of respondents indicate that they use at least one of the PLA methods listed in the survey instrument. Respondents tend to use quantitative methods of PLA (CLEP, AP, ACT/PEP, DANTES and Course Challenge) more frequently than the use of qualitative measures (ACE PONSI/CREDIT and military and Individual Assessment).

Prior Learning Assessment Methods Used

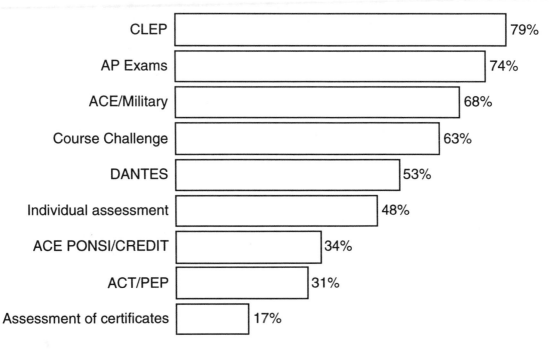

Method	Percent
CLEP	79%
AP Exams	74%
ACE/Military	68%
Course Challenge	63%
DANTES	53%
Individual assessment	48%
ACE PONSI/CREDIT	34%
ACT/PEP	31%
Assessment of certificates	17%

To explore the differences among institutions using the various PLA methods, respondents were examined according to their institutional characteristics and their PLA preferences. *(See the table below and Appendix C for detailed comparisons by the PLA methods.)*

PLA Category by Institutional Characteristics

	Any PLA	Standardized	Challenge	Guidelines	Individual Assessment
Public	95%	94%	79%	81%	49%
Private	86%	82%	54%	62%	53%
Carnegie Classification					
Associate's	95%	93%	81%	79%	56%
Bachelor's	95%	94%	56%	71%	54%
Master's	98%	98%	75%	87%	62%
Doctorate	98%	98%	68%	64%	39%
Research	88%	81%	68%	51%	26%
Specific/other	57%	45%	33%	36%	31%
Region (Census)					
East North Central	88%	85%	58%	65%	57%
East South Central	89%	89%	61%	77%	38%
Mountain	84%	92%	77%	77%	46%
Mid Atlantic	90%	87%	61%	64%	58%
North East	88%	84%	52%	65%	61%
Pacific	78%	72%	61%	61%	46%
South Atlantic	95%	91%	64%	73%	43%
West North Central	89%	87%	69%	77%	50%
West South Central	90%	88%	76%	74%	44%
Region (Accrediting Agency)					
Middle States	90%	87%	61%	64%	55%
North Central	89%	87%	65%	70%	54%
New England	88%	85%	52%	66%	62%
Northwest	87%	85%	70%	76%	44%
Western	73%	67%	52%	53%	39%
Southern	91%	88%	68%	73%	41%
Other	94%	94%	56%	69%	41%
Total enrollment					
Less than 1,000 students	72%	64%	38%	48%	44%
1,001 to 5,000 students	94%	92%	68%	75%	53%
Above 5,000 students	97%	96%	78%	78%	51%
Percent minority students					
Between 1–10% Minority	91%	89%	64%	72%	52%
Between 10–20% Minority	88%	85%	63%	69%	50%
Above 20% Minority	85%	82%	61%	62%	45%
Percent non-traditional students					
0–7% Non-traditional students	68%	60%	31%	32%	23%
7.1%–17% Non-traditional students	96%	94%	69%	77%	50%
17%–28% Non-traditional students	96%	95%	75%	84%	58%
Above 28% Non-traditional students	94%	92%	75%	80%	67%

Examining the use of PLA in this way reveals that most institutions use standardized PLA methods while fewer institutions use challenge exams and guidelines for assessment and far fewer use individual assessment methods.

Standardized exams are used by a greater percentage of institutions than any other PLA category, regardless of the institution's size, location or makeup. This finding may be attributable, in part, to the fact that standardized exams are likely to be the most convenient way for an institution to assess students' knowledge, skills and abilities, since the administration, including creating, testing, and scoring the exam, is done by an outside testing organization rather than the institution.

While challenge PLA exams require greater effort by the institution to develop, maintain, and administer, the data show that a majority of institutions offer this type of PLA method (with the exception of small, atypical institutions with small minority populations).

General observations of the use of PLA by institutional characteristics include the following: *(See Appendix C for the table illustrating these findings)*:

- ◆ A greater percentage of public institutions use standardized exams (such as AP, CLEP, DANTES), challenge exams and guideline assessment (such as the ACE armed forces guidelines) than do private institutions. Standardized exams are still the most prevalent form, private institutions; however, are more likely to use individual assessment than their public counterparts.

- ◆ A greater percentage of doctoral, master's, bachelor's and associate's institutions (Carnegie Classifications) use PLA methods than do Research and Specialized/other specified institutions. (Note: Carnegie Classification indicates the highest degree offered, not the only degree. In addition, particular degree granting institutions may offer PLA at some degree levels and not others.)

- ◆ A greater percentage (between approximately 20 and 30 percentage points) of mid-size (1,001 to 5,000 students) and large (above 5,000) institutions use a broader range of the PLA methods than smaller institutions (except individual portfolio assessment).

- ◆ A greater percentage of institutions with fewer minority students (between 1–10 percent) use a broader range of the PLA methods than those institutions with a higher percentage of minority students (above 20 percent).

- ◆ A greater percentage of institutions with a larger proportion of non-traditional aged students use a broader range of the PLA methods than those institutions with smaller non-traditional aged populations.

- ◆ Overall, the use of a variety of PLA methods appears to increase as student diversity increases. This includes diversity in both ethnic mix and age of the student body.

Chapter 4
PLA Policies and Procedures: Methods of PLA

PLA Administration

The existence of a central office for PLA can be regarded as a fundamental step toward institutionalizing the assessment of prior learning on an individual campus. A central office for prior learning may facilitate students' efforts to obtain information about PLA and may increase the likelihood that policies and procedures are maintained and applied consistently.

Over three-fourths of the responding institutions offering some form of PLA maintain a central office for the administration and assessment of prior learning. Half of these institutions conduct PLA affairs from their existing registrar's office and the remaining conduct PLA through their continuing or adult education offices or admissions offices.

Location of PLA Advising Function

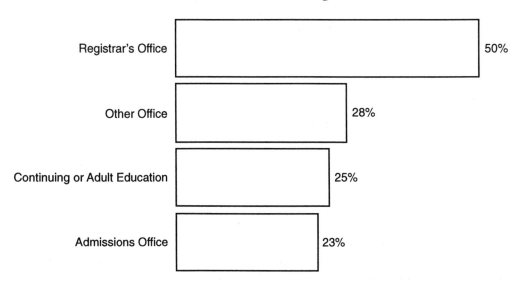

Registrar's Office — 50%

Other Office — 28%

Continuing or Adult Education — 25%

Admissions Office — 23%

In 1991 a similar proportion of institutions provided a central office for the administration and assessment of PLA. In addition, a similar proportion located this central office within their existing registrar's office.

A majority of the institutions maintain policies and procedures to facilitate students' use and application of PLA toward course or degree requirements. For instance, most institutions (72 percent) offer advising and assistance for students in pursuit of PLA recognition and credit. Nearly as many institutions maintain written guidelines for students to follow in pursuing credit for PLA. In addition, over half of the responding institutions using PLA offer procedures for students to add information to their portfolio after the request for PLA credit has been filed or to appeal their request after it has been denied.

The following chart illustrates the extent to which student-friendly policies and procedures are used by responding institutions.

Administration Procedures for PLA

Credit given for PLA is equivalent to course credit	75%
Advising and assistance are available	72%
Written guidelines for students are maintained	63%
Procedures for students to add information are provided	58%
Appeal procedures are provided	56%
Assessor interview is required	34%
School determines credit request	49%
Student determines credit request	32%

PLA Assessment Process

An institution's timing of prior learning assessment and the duration of the PLA opportunity speak to issues of institutional resources and capacity for assessment as well as student-friendly policies and procedures. Forty percent of the responding institutions allow for prior learning assessment both before and after enrollment, while one-third of the institutions (33 percent) limit prior learning assessment until after the student has enrolled. A smaller percentage of institutions require prior learning to be assessed prior to enrollment (5 percent) or after the first year of instruction (4 percent). Twelve percent of the institutions have designated prior learning assessment faculty or staff, while over sixty percent rely on faculty in the specific department of the assessment or credit request.

Some institutions charge fees for PLA to defray the costs associated with assessment training, time to conduct the assessment and the maintenance and upkeep of an assessment program or institutional policies and procedures. Fees for PLA are applied at institutions in various ways, ranging from posting and evaluation fees to tuition costs for a portfolio development course. The breakdown of assessment fees among responding institutions is illustrated in the following chart.

Assessment Fees

Evaluation fees	35%
Tuition for portfolio development course	23%
Posting fees	15%
Other	11%

Procedures for Awarding PLA Credit[7]

A majority of institutions offering PLA, maintain policies for governing the award of prior learning credit for each of the assessment methods *(See chart below)*.

Nearly all institutions that award credit using standardized exams or challenge exams to assess prior learning require a minimum level of proficiency for the award of credit. Some institutions maintain policies regarding the maximum number of prior learning assessment credits possible per student. Not only does the proficiency standard ensure consistency across the board, it makes the administration of PLA easier for the institution.

Policies Exist That Govern the Award of Credit by PLA Method

CLEP	90%
AP	88%
DANTES	80%
Challenge exams	79%
ACT/PEP	78%
ACE/Military	75%
Individual Assessment	72%
ACE PONSI/CREDIT	72%

[7] Note that most charts related to institutional PLA administration policy exclude the PLA method of assessment of certificates. The 1996 Survey of Prior Learning Assessment did not consistently ask each policy question for each of the PLA methods. Thus assessment of certificates is excluded in those instances where there is no data.

Because students' knowledge, skills and abilities vary among departments and by field of study, some institutions allow their prior learning assessment policies to vary across these dimensions as well.

Permitting such variation across departments or levels within the institution allows individual departments at institutions a greater degree of independence in assessing the individual student's request. Depending on how these variations by department or institutional level are monitored, they may result in a more authentic examination of the student's experience and thus, a more accurate assessment.

Greater variation in administration is given for challenge exams, with less variation for DANTES, CLEP, and other forms of assessment.

Among other policies that concern PLA at institutions are those that govern the maximum number of credits that may be awarded.

Policies Exist for Maximum Credit Award

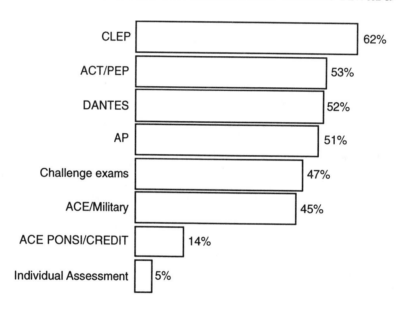

CLEP	62%
ACT/PEP	53%
DANTES	52%
AP	51%
Challenge exams	47%
ACE/Military	45%
ACE PONSI/CREDIT	14%
Individual Assessment	5%

Credit Awarded by Degree Type

The data in the following charts illustrate the application of credit for prior learning policy at institutions according to their Carnegie Classification. Fewer institutions conferring higher level awards offer PLA credit at the higher degree levels (e.g., doctorate or master's). For instance, only 6 percent of institutions that confer master's degrees apply PLA credit at the master's level.

This finding may reflect the market demand for PLA and the demographic profile of students at the associate's degree and bachelor's degree level, where students are seeking education and training to: 1) upgrade their skills; 2) change career paths; or 3) obtain credentials or proof of the knowledge, skills and abilities attained in a particular field.

In addition, this finding may reflect a perceived difference in education and training standards between the undergraduate and graduate levels. For instance, education and training attained at the higher degree levels may be regarded as more specialized, and more focused on theory, research, and higher order thinking skills, rather than on fundamental knowledge and skill-building as developed at the associate's and bachelor's level.

PLA Credit Applied Toward Degree
By Highest Level of Degree Offered

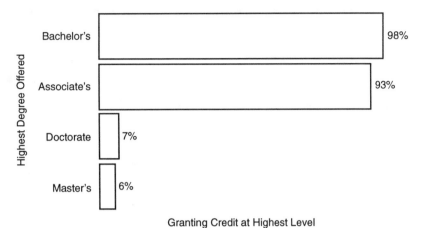

An external factor influencing this finding is that some of the American regional accrediting agencies pressure institutions to severely restrict the award of credit that may be transferred into graduate programs, regardless of the credit sources (including graduate-level courses taken at other institutions). The rationale for these restrictions is frequently described in terms of maintaining the quality and integrity of graduate programs, even though institutions are equally accountable in this regard for their undergraduate programs.

On the other hand, a greater percentage of institutions granting higher level degrees do recognize and grant credit for prior learning at lower degree levels such as an associate's or a bachelor's degree level (as opposed to a master's or a doctorate degree). The following charts illustrate institution's policy with regard to basic degree requirements as well as major and minor degree requirements according to the institution's Carnegie Classification.

The charts below and on the following page illustrate the ways in which PLA credit is applied by the highest level of degree conferred at the institution.

PLA Applied Toward General Education
By Highest Level of Degree Conferred

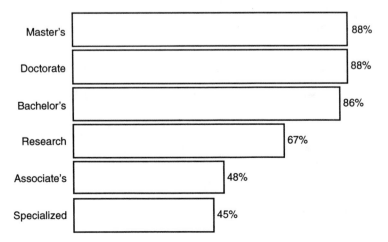

PLA Applied Toward Major Requirements
By Highest Level of Degree Conferred

Master's	80%
Doctorate	79%
Bachelor's	78%
Research	50%
Associate's	43%
Specialized	37%

PLA Applied Toward Minor Requirements
By Highest Level of Degree Conferred

Master's	77%
Doctorate	76%
Bachelor's	72%
Research	51%
Specialized	26%
Associate's	23%

Documenting PLA

How an institution documents a student's prior learning on the student's transcript is as important to the student as the policies for awarding credit for prior learning. A student seeking to advance his or her career through formal academic recognition of knowledge and skills may rely on a college's assessment of this knowledge and these skills. Thus, the way in which the assessed credit award is documented could affect the student's academic career and job status.

The following chart illustrates how responding institutions recognize and document PLA on students' transcripts. A majority of the institutions list both the course title and document that that credit was earned for the student's prior learning.

Issuance of PLA Credit on Transcript

Course title listed	68%
Indication that credit was earned	52%
Indication within a block of credits earned	14%
No course title listed	11%
No indication that credit was earned	7%

Chapter 5
Changes in PLA Use Over Time

In comparing the 1996 sample of respondents to the 1991 sample, two new data sets of 614 respondents were created. These new data sets represent subsets of the total respondents for both years and include only those institutions that participated both in 1991 and in the 1996 surveys. The following table illustrates the percent of institutions using each PLA option in both 1991 and 1996.

Changes in PLA Use: 1991 and 1996

	1991	1996*
Standardized		
Advanced Placement	90% N=614	92% N=592
CLEP	88% N=614	89% N=596
ACT/PEP	35% N=614	37% N=586
DANTES	52% N=614	62% N=585
Challenge		
Challenge Exam	72% N=614	72% N=591
Guidelines		
ACE PONSI/CREDIT	33% N=614	43% N=588
ACE/Military	75% N=614	78% N=594
*Individual Assessment***		
Individual assessment	50% N=614	55% N=595

*Because respondents to the 1996 survey missed or skipped questions frequently throughout the questionnaire, numerical comparisons between the two years are not made and the sample size across items vary.

**Assessment of certificates is not included among the PLA methods comparison between 1991 and 1996, because this method was not reported in the Prior Learning Assessment Survey published in 1992.

In comparing PLA use among respondents who participated in both surveys, it is evident that the use of PLA increased proportionally across most of the PLA methods. Respondents' use of DANTES, ACE/PONSI and Individual Assessment appear to be increasing proportionally faster with a greater percentage using these options in 1996 than in 1991, as compared to the other PLA methods.

On the surface these increases do not appear to be systematic, as these PLA methods cover the range of types from standardized exams to individual assessment.

Chapter 6
Best Practices of PLA

Best practices are not always those that are demonstrated most frequently; nonetheless, it is important to understand who is using PLA and which methods are most prevalent. In this way, advocates of PLA may identify particular profiles of institutions that are ready to expand or refine their PLA offerings, and institutions can assess how close or how far their use or non-use of given PLA methods are from the mainstream. The data from this study do not reveal which methods of PLA are necessarily the "best" methods either for institutions or for students, but the findings do suggest the kinds of issues that must be addressed in such a study to discover "best practices" in PLA.

Overall, it appears that institutions favor PLA methods (especially testing) that are quantitatively based, require minimal institutional effort, and present academic-based demonstrations of students' knowledge, skills, and abilities. Institutions probably favor these approaches because of the methods' convenience, consistency, and administrative simplicity. Each institution will select and support PLA methods appropriate to its mission and purposes, so the first question is, "Which methods of PLA are best for this institution?" Framed in this way, the question is likely to be answered from a perspective that values efficiency and economy to the institution.

However, that first question might also be posed to ask, "Which methods of PLA are best for the students of this institution?" This latter formulation points to complex issues surrounding recognition and respect given students' pre-college experiences, due process in deciding the creditworthiness of student learning, and the importance of individuation (as opposed to standardization) when dealing with students. These and other complexities that flow from a student-centered perspective on PLA indicate that externally developed standardized tests and internally-derived challenge exams make the search for "best practices" quite different for testing compared to other PLA methods. Best practices for testing largely have to do with adhering to test developers' advice on such matters as proctoring, secure storage, and cut-scores, while best practices for individualized PLA methods (like portfolio assessment) must address matters such as student advising/motivation, faculty preparation, and adjudication of disputed or ambiguous cases.

Regardless of which PLA method is viewed, best practice can only be built upon a foundation that respects standards of quality assurance, among them:

- Credit should be awarded only for college-level learning
- Competence levels and credit awards should be made only by subject matter experts
- Credit should be awarded only in the context appropriate for it
- Credit should not be given twice for the same learning
- Full disclosure should be made of policies and procedures used
- Assessors need adequate training on an on-going basis

(These and other standards are discussed in Urban Whitaker's *Assessing Learning: Standards, Principles, & Procedures*).

Chapter 7
The Challenges of PLA

An institution's policies and procedures for recognizing and awarding credit for prior learning determine the nature of students' experience and students' potential for success with the assessment process. In determining PLA policies and procedures, institutions must consider a variety of issues. Among these are institutional resources and assessment capacity as well as financial considerations.

With the nature of the student body at many institutions becoming older, more diverse, and part-time, the non-traditional student market has exploded. These students often come to the institutions with a variety of life experiences and skills as well as expectations that these experiences can be translated into academic experiences. As competition for these students continues to increase, institutions are responding with vast changes in their recruitment strategies, their prior learning assessment policies, their curricula and instructional strategies, and their student support services, to name only a few. Such changes are aimed at recruiting students, maintaining competitive advantage and securing tuition revenue.

An institution's resources and capacity for assessment help shape, in part, its policies and procedures for PLA. An institution may feel constrained by its human resources and thus formulate its PLA policies and procedures accordingly. These policies and procedures, however, may have long-term impact on enrollment and tuition revenue.

If an institution's PLA policies and procedures contribute to students not completing their programs, the loss of potential tuition is costly. If, however, prior learning credits are offered for courses, the marginal up-front losses in revenue for these courses is quickly offset by the students' matriculation and retention to program completion. Such issues are considerations for institutions in determining the appropriate PLA methods in light of its enrollment and educational strategies.

While these represent only a few of the issues that an institution may consider in determining prior learning assessment policy and procedures, they demonstrate the complexity of the issues at hand.

Chapter 8
Future Research

The 1996 survey profiled the incidence of various PLA practices among more than 1,100 colleges and universities. Innumerable questions remain concerning the use and impact of PLA to fully understand which kinds of PLA activities are most prevalent and how such programs are administered. The following discussion identifies some of these issues and the opportunity for future research.

Creating a Projectable Sample

In conducting future research it is highly desirable to attain a true probability sample that is fully representative of the universe of accredited colleges and universities. Toward that end, it is desirable to administer a future survey—again administered to all accredited colleges and universities but with more rigorous record control and multiple follow-up waves to achieve a fully projectable sample. With respect to design, one of the most fundamental questions is simply whether an institution utilizes PLA at all. Towards that end, consideration may be given to a design that would quickly identify institutions not using PLA.

Moving from Incidence to Impact

The 1991 and 1996 surveys tracked in considerable detail whether colleges used PLA using various methods. At the same time, however, questions concerning how many students were affected by PLA policies or how many credits awarded through PLA were not considered. A logical extension to the prior surveys would be the addition of questions such as: 1) Number of students who sought PLA credit recognition 2) Number of students awarded. 3) Number of PLA credits generated. Taking these questions one step further would entail an inquiry into what the outcomes and impact of PLA on students.

Clarifying Motivations

From both a student and institutional perspective, PLA creates opportunities. From a representative sample of PLA recipients, future research could examine in greater detail the motivations of both institutions and students in using PLA. This would include an examination of users versus non-users to clarify strategies of using PLA.

Related Issues

Two aspects of PLA play against a larger landscape of a changing market. First, PLA continues to exist within a broader context of learning assessment, in general, which continues to evolve. Secondly, PLA exists in the midst of and may be challenged by the continual expansion of unconventional education providers such as Web and media based learning. How institutions will make sense of these will pivot, in large part, on policies related to assessment in general and PLA in particular.

Future Inquiry

CAEL encourages and invites researchers and institutions to approach CAEL for more information about PLA, the research presented herein or for access to the database and data set used for this report.

Appendix A

Report and Survey Methodology

Methodology[8]

SURVEY INSTRUMENT

The following section presents the methodology used to gather the information found in the data set used for this report. Included are brief descriptions of the sample, the prior learning assessment survey, and the procedures used to gather the data.

National Sample

Data collection was conducted through the use of a mailed paper and pencil instrument with return postage, supported by a second mailing with telephone reminders to a selected sample. The initial sample utilized a mailing list provided by CAEL consisting of 2,421 institutions previously identified as utilizing prior learning assessment. In most cases, a specific individual knowledgeable of prior learning assessment at the institution was identified.

A first mailing to all sampling units was conducted in June 1996; a total of 1,069 useable responses were obtained by August 1996. A second mailing to all non-respondents was conducted in August 1996 yielding 112 additional responses.

Purposive Sampling

Two purposive sampling activities were conducted to support formation of the data set for the Prior Learning Assessment Survey. CAEL staff reviewed the list of institutions responding to the paper-pencil instrument and identified two samples for follow-up contact. The first purposive sample represented all institutions having a member on the Board of CAEL. A copy of the instrument was sent to the list of board members supplied by CAEL (n=25) with a request that they complete the survey or forward it to their appropriate institutional representative. The second purposive sample also reflected CAEL membership. At

---

[8] Note: Appendix A was derived from the "Project Overview" prepared by the Evaluation Consortium for the survey on "Current Practices in Adult Learning, Practices in Prior Learning Assessment (1996)."

the time of the second mailing, CAEL staff conducted a review of institutions responding to the survey and identified a selected sub sample of non-respondents (n=29) who held membership in CAEL but who had not yet responded to the survey. As part of the second mailing, representatives of these purposive samples were first contacted by telephone, informed of the importance of the survey and the information. This telephone contact was followed by a second mailing of the survey.

Instrumentation

The Current Practices in Prior Learning Assessment Survey addressed three areas: 1) types of prior learning assessment accepted by the institution; 2) administration of and procedures related to conducting prior learning assessment at that institution; and, 3) institutional policies governing transfer of prior learning assessment credits from other institutions. A summation of each of these sections is presented below.

Types of Prior Learning Assessment

This section of the survey addressed methods and types of prior learning assessment conducted at the responding institution. Nine methods of assessing prior learning and/or experiences were included:

- Credit for achievement on Advanced Placement tests;
- Credit for appropriate scores on College Level Examination Program (CLEP) exams;
- Credit for appropriate scores on the American College Testing Proficiency Examination Program;
- Course Challenge/Department Examinations;
- Credit recommendations of the American Council on Education (ACE) Program on Non-Collegiate Sponsored Instruction (PONSI);
- Credit recommendations of the American Council on Education (ACE) Guide to the Evaluation of Education Experiences in the Armed Services;
- Individual Prior Learning Assessment; and
- Evaluation of local training programs

For each of these methods, information was obtained on the following:

- use at the institution,
- minimal value representing acceptability,
- presence of policies at the department and institutional level, and
- variations in policy.

The number of items utilized for each type of credit varied between 5 and 23. A check list approach utilizing a binomial choice of "yes" and "no" was provided for response to survey items.

Administration of and Procedures for Prior Learning Assessment

This section of the survey addressed administrative policy for prior learning assessment. Specific questions addressed the presence of a central office related to prior learning assessment; the presence of written guidelines for prior learning assessment; the status of persons doing the actual assessment and making the recommendations for acceptance; the nature of training for prior learning assessment staff; the procedures related to use of transcripts; time of assessment, and fee structure; and the approximate number of students and credits involved in prior learning assessment on an annual basis. As in the prior section, the majority of items were of a check list nature utilizing an option of "yes" or "no."

Policies Governing Transfer of Credits from Other Institutions

The third section of the Prior Learning Assessment Survey gathered data pertaining to policies and procedures used by the responding institution when, through prior learning assessment, they awarded credits earned from other institutions. Questions addressed in this section include: acceptance of prior learning credits granted by other institutions, limitations to acceptance, and presence of written policies and procedures related to this acceptance. The majority of these questions received binomial "yes" or "no" responses. Qualitative procedural responses were coded to reflect summary information.

ADMINISTRATION PROCEDURES

Sampling Frame

A purposive sampling frame was utilized to solicit responses for the Prior Learning Assessment Survey. The overall sample, provided by CAEL, consisted of 2,241 institutions of higher education with known programs in adult and experiential learning. In addition, two sub-samples were identified by CAEL staff for inclusion in a separate phone contact.

Initial Development of the Survey

Initial development and design of concepts for the Prior Learning Assessment Survey was conducted by the Council for Adult and Experiential Learning. A draft survey was prepared by CAEL staff and forwarded to the Evaluation Consortium for review and preparation. Upon receipt of the survey, Consortium staff reviewed the document for measurement visibility, language and literacy level, and coding format. Where necessary, items were reworded to meet consistent language and literacy levels, discrete outcomes, and progressive responses. Presentation of items and methods of responses were reformatted to increase response motivation and ease of completion. The changes were reviewed by CAEL staff and their suggestions integrated into the pre-validated form of the survey.

Survey Validation

As part of the design and validation of the instrument, three nationally known experts in the fields of higher education and educational assessment reviewed and assisted in the revision of the instrument. Two of the reviewers reflected expert knowledge in the field of higher education and research, especially as it relates to adult learning.

The first, Dr. Joan Knapp of Knapp and Associates International, Inc. in Princeton, New Jersey, was selected as a specialist in prior learning assessment and was asked to validate the scale in terms of the content and acceptability of response options. The second reviewer, Dr. William Husson, Academic Dean of Regis University in Denver, Colorado, provided input on the generalizability of the Prior Learning Assessment Survey to researchers interested in the administration, design implementation, and outcomes of adult education. The third reviewer was Dr. Robert McMorris, a specialist in educational assessment and evaluation. Dr. McMorris is experienced in survey design and development, as it is related to programmatic and institutional settings, as well as possessing technical knowledge of instrument design and analysis. Drafts of the instrument were provided to the expert panel for review and suggested revisions as well as feedback on content and logical construct validity. Specific feedback from the validators was used to modify individual items and instructions to represent institutional programmatic uses. Where inconsistent recommendations were offered, or where variations from standard measurement practices (e.g., length of instrument) were noted, the changes were reviewed with NLL staff for final decision on the inclusion or alteration. These alterations resulted in an instrument ready for piloting with a selected group of respondents.

Pilot of the Prior Learning Assessment Survey

Six institutions of higher education were selected to serve as pilot recipients of the survey. Names and addresses of the institutions, and the name of a contact person at each site were provided by Nation of Lifelong Learners' staff. Each of these representatives was contacted via telephone and asked to participate in the sample. Respondents were informed of the purpose of the survey, asked to complete the survey or forward it to an appropriate person at their institution for completion, and requested to provide any feedback relevant to the completion. Pilot responses were obtained from 4 of the 6 pilot institutions. (One respondent was unable to review the material for personal reasons. One respondent indicated that the survey was too long and chose to not continue with the process.) Suggested responses were reviewed by Consortium staff and were implemented where feasible. After the survey was formatted for final printing, it was reviewed by NLL/CAEL staff and prepared for mailing.

Data Collection for the Prior Learning Assessment Survey

As indicated above, two major mailings were conducted for the Prior Learning Assessment Survey. The first mailing was sent in June 1996 to representatives of 2,421 institutions of higher education, with specific selection of sample units designated by the Council for Adult and Experiential Learning. A second mailing (n=1,352) was sent to non-respondents in August 1996. Two additional purposive samples, selected by the CAEL staff, were included in a follow-up mailing.

MERGED DATA WITH INTEGRATED POSTSECONDARY EDUCATION DATA SYSTEM (IPEDS)

To provide a more full and complete analysis, the 1996 survey data was merged/combined with the IPEDS public data set. The IPEDS provides detailed information regarding an institution's enrollment; degrees conferred; various institutional characteristics; and financial status including specific revenues and expenditures. In the merge process, incomplete surveys, surveys with incorrect institutional information or incomplete IPEDS information were excluded. Thus, the analysis included herein includes a total of 1,135 institutions (approximately 47 percent of the population of institutions invited to participate).

At the time of preparation of this report for publication, the original address file for those institutions that were invited to participate is not available. Therefore, precise response rates by institutional characteristics (type of institution or by geographic region) are not possible. In other words, this report is limited to outlining, in a simple and straightforward manner, who responded to the survey and how. In the few cases when additional information or data *is* available either through the 1991 CAEL Survey of Prior Learning Assessment or other CAEL documentation, comparisons with the population of accredited institutions and changes over time (1991 to 1996) are noted.

LIMITATIONS OF THE DATA SET

As mentioned in the text of the report, the data set is limited due to a variety of constraints. First and foremost, the original documentation regarding the population of institution is unavailable (at the time of preparation of this report). This limits the precise calculation of response rates and response rates by institutional characteristics. It also limits weighting the data by institutional characteristic so that the sample of responding institutions (1,135) reflects the total population of institutions according to these characteristics.

To circumvent these limitations, we have carefully constructed several data sets including the 1991 and 1996 subsets of respondents as well as the 1995–1996 IPEDS data set of accredited postsecondary institutions. These data sets are used to make comparisons and as a surrogate measure of representatives of the 1996 sample of respondents to the population of accredited institutions as a whole. It is important to note that due to the limitations posed by the administration of the 1996 survey, comparisons and generalizations made throughout the report could not be based upon precise methodology.

The low response rate is also a constraining factor. Higher response rates would increase the likelihood that the information gathered was representative of the total population of institutions. In addition, the purposive sampling design limits the analysis in that those not known to use PLA were not sampled, thus more advanced statistical analyses were not possible.

The questionnaire design is also problematic. The format of the questionnaire is complex. From our examination of individual institutional responses it appears that some of the respondents became confused by or impatient with the questions as designed, leading to some inaccuracies or inconsistencies in individuals' responses. As a result, the 1996 surveys may have a higher proportion of missing data making comparison to the 1991 data less precise or meaningful.

Definitions

Carnegie Classifications[9]

Associates of Arts Colleges: These institutions offer associates of arts certificate or degree programs and, with a few exceptions, offer no baccalaureate degrees.

Baccalaureate Colleges (I and II):   These institutions are primarily undergraduate colleges with major emphasis on baccalaureate degree programs. They award 40 percent or more of their baccalaureate degrees in liberal arts fields and cover a range of levels of restriction in admissions.

Master's Colleges and Universities: These institutions offer a full range of baccalaureate programs and are committed to graduate education through the master's degree. They award 20 or more master's degrees annually in one or more disciplines.

Doctoral Universities (I and II):   These institutions offer a full range of baccalaureate programs and are committed to graduate education through the doctorate. They award between 10–40 doctoral degrees annually between three to five or more disciplines.

Research Universities (I and II):   These institutions offer a full range of baccalaureates programs, are committed to graduate education through the doctorate, and give high priority to research. They award 50 or more doctoral degrees each year. In addition, they received annually between $15.5 million and $40 million in federal support.

Specialized/Other: These institutions offer degrees ranging from the bachelor's to the doctorate. At least 50 percent of the degrees awarded by these institutions are in a single discipline. This category also includes institutions that award most of their degrees in such fields as chiropractic, nursing, pharmacy, or podiatry.

---

[9] The Carnegie Foundation for the Advancement of Teaching: A Classification of Institutions of Higher Education, 1994 Edition, pp. 15–17.

CENSUS REGION CLASSIFICATIONS[10]

Pacific: AK, WA, OR, CA

Mountain: NV, MT, ID, WY, UT, CO, AZ, NM

West North Central: ND, MN, SD, NE, IA, KS, MO

West South Central: OK, AR, TX, LA

East North Central: WI, MI, IL, IN, OH

East South Central: KY, TN, MS, AL

Mid-Atlantic: NY, PA, NJ

South Atlantic: WV, DE, MD, VA, NC, SC, GA, FL

New England: ME, VT, NH, MA, CT, RI

ACCREDITING AGENCY REGIONS

Middle States Association Region: DE, DC, MD, NJ, NY, PA, Puerto Rico, Virgin Islands

New England Association Region: CT, ME, MA, NH, VT, RI

North Central Association Region: AZ, AR, CO, IL, IN, IA, KS, MI, MN, MO, NE, NM, ND, OH, OK, SD, WV, WI, WY

Northwest Association Region: AK, ID, MT, NV, OR , UT, WA

Southern Association Region: AL, FL, GE, KT, LA, MS, NC, SC, TN, TX, VA

Western Association Region: CA, HI, American Samoa, Guam

---

[10] Source: U.S. Census Bureau

Appendix B

Comparisons with 1992 Survey of Prior Learning Assessment

Comparison of Participation by State 1991 and 1996

State	Total		1991	91 Percent of Total	1996	96 Percent of Total	Comparison with 1992
AL	82	2.22%	35	2.04%	19	1.67%	−16
AK	11	0.30%	3	0.17%	2	0.18%	−1
AZ	45	1.22%	16	0.93%	10	0.88%	−6
AR	35	0.95%	14	0.81%	13	1.14%	−1
CA	351	9.51%	123	7.16%	59	5.19%	−64
CO	59	1.60%	28	1.63%	12	1.06%	−16
CT	51	1.38%	21	1.22%	16	1.41%	−5
DE	12	0.33%	4	0.23%	1	0.09%	−3
FL	94	2.55%	52	3.03%	25	2.20%	−27
GA	89	2.41%	45	2.62%	24	2.11%	−21
HI	16	0.43%	2	0.12%	4	0.35%	2
ID	11	0.30%	7	0.41%	4	0.35%	−3
IL	181	4.90%	85	4.95%	61	5.36%	−24
IN	79	2.14%	43	2.50%	36	3.17%	−7
IA	63	1.71%	40	2.33%	28	2.46%	−12
KS	54	1.46%	33	1.92%	27	2.37%	−6
KY	65	1.76%	37	2.15%	20	1.76%	−17
LA	38	1.03%	16	0.93%	10	0.88%	−6
ME	31	0.84%	12	0.70%	9	0.79%	−3
MD	61	1.65%	24	1.40%	22	1.93%	−2
MA	120	3.25%	57	3.32%	41	3.61%	−16
MI	97	2.63%	57	3.32%	39	3.43%	−18
MN	71	1.92%	37	2.15%	25	2.20%	−12
MS	42	1.14%	21	1.22%	6	0.53%	−15
MO	99	2.68%	52	3.03%	29	2.55%	−23
MT	20	0.54%	8	0.47%	10	0.88%	2
NE	34	0.92%	21	1.22%	13	1.14%	−8
NV	11	0.30%	1	0.06%	1	0.09%	0
NH	27	0.73%	11	0.64%	9	0.79%	−2
NJ	66	1.79%	28	1.63%	16	1.41%	−12
NM	25	0.68%	15	0.87%	8	0.70%	−7
NY	307	8.32%	105	6.11%	83	7.30%	−22
NC	125	3.39%	70	4.07%	47	4.13%	−23
ND	22	0.60%	13	0.76%	8	0.70%	−5
OH	145	3.93%	84	4.89%	58	5.10%	−26
OK	47	1.27%	20	1.16%	7	0.62%	−13
OR	48	1.30%	30	1.75%	24	2.11%	−6
PA	216	5.85%	90	5.24%	74	6.51%	−16
RI	11	0.30%	4	0.23%	1	0.09%	−3
SC	66	1.79%	33	1.92%	16	1.41%	−17
SD	23	0.62%	14	0.81%	11	0.97%	−3
TN	87	2.36%	42	2.44%	28	2.46%	−14
TX	191	5.17%	82	4.77%	57	5.01%	−25
UT	16	0.43%	8	0.47%	6	0.53%	−2
VT	26	0.70%	15	0.87%	7	0.62%	−8
VA	80	2.17%	46	2.68%	21	1.85%	−25
WA	60	1.63%	37	2.15%	23	2.02%	−14
WV	29	0.79%	15	0.87%	7	0.62%	−8
WI	66	1.79%	36	2.10%	36	3.17%	0
WY	9	0.24%	4	0.23%		0.00%	−4
DC	17	0.46%	7	0.41%	4	0.35%	−3
Samoa	1	0.03%	1	0.06%		0.00%	−1
Guam	2	0.05%	1	0.06%		0.00%	−1
Mariana	1	0.03%	0	0.00%		0.00%	0
Micronesia	3	0.08%	0	0.00%		0.00%	0
PR	52	1.41%	12	0.70%	10	0.88%	−2
VI	1	0.03%	1	0.06%		0.00%	−1
Missing	0	0.00%	0	0.00%	10	0.88%	10
Total	**3691**	**100.00%**	**1718**	**100.00%**	**1137**	**100.00%**	

Appendix C

PLA
by Institutional Characteristics

Prior Learning Assessment by Institutional Characteristics

	Any PLA	AP	CLEP	ACT/PEP	DANTES	Challenge	ACE PONSI/CRDT	ACE/Military	Ind. Assess.	Assmnt. of cert.
Public	95%	84%	92%	32%	64%	82%	34%	83%	46%	21%
Private	86%	79%	80%	35%	54%	59%	41%	67%	56%	18%
Carnegie Classification										
Associate's	95%	78%	91%	32%	60%	83%	32%	81%	51%	30%
Bachelor's	95%	89%	85%	34%	60%	58%	44%	72%	56%	17%
Master's	98%	90%	97%	46%	67%	77%	47%	87%	60%	19%
Doctorate	98%	98%	88%	27%	60%	71%	29%	67%	39%	9%
Research	88%	74%	74%	21%	46%	72%	27%	54%	28%	6%
Specific/other	57%	43%	50%	21%	33%	43%	22%	44%	37%	12%
Region (Census)										
East North Central	88%	77%	83%	33%	54%	63%	35%	68%	58%	22%
East South Central	89%	94%	91%	31%	59%	68%	44%	82%	39%	14%
Mountain	84%	84%	90%	34%	66%	78%	41%	83%	43%	22%
Mid-Atlantic	90%	82%	87%	44%	58%	65%	44%	66%	58%	20%
North East	88%	77%	82%	45%	61%	57%	50%	71%	64%	24%
Pacific	78%	68%	66%	21%	50%	68%	34%	68%	47%	11%
South Atlantic	95%	83%	88%	22%	60%	67%	33%	74%	42%	21%
West North Central	89%	78%	87%	39%	63%	72%	34%	80%	52%	17%
West South Central	90%	84%	90%	35%	49%	81%	31%	76%	43%	19%
Region (Accred. Agency)										
Middle States	90%	82%	85%	43%	56%	65%	42%	66%	56%	19%
North Central	89%	79%	85%	36%	58%	68%	36%	74%	55%	22%
New England	88%	76%	82%	44%	61%	58%	51%	71%	64%	25%
Northwest	88%	80%	81%	21%	53%	73%	38%	79%	43%	11%
Western	73%	67%	60%	19%	50%	60%	27%	62%	40%	13%
Southern	91%	84%	88%	27%	57%	73%	33%	77%	41%	17%
Other	94%	84%	91%	16%	56%	56%	31%	69%	41%	10%
Total enrollment										
Less than 1,000 students	72%	65%	66%	22%	44%	44%	31%	55%	49%	13%
1,001 to 5,000 students	94%	84%	88%	37%	59%	72%	41%	78%	52%	19%
Above 5,000 students	97%	86%	92%	37%	65%	80%	37%	79%	49%	24%
Percent minority students										
Between 1–10% Minority	91%	83%	88%	35%	59%	68%	41%	75%	53%	18%
Between 10–20% Minority	88%	79%	82%	36%	54%	68%	37%	74%	51%	20%
Above 20% Minority	85%	75%	79%	26%	56%	65%	28%	65%	44%	19%
Percent non-traditional										
0–7%	68%	66%	51%	13%	24%	38%	16%	37%	27%	4%
7.1%–17%	96%	91%	92%	36%	59%	72%	37%	78%	50%	13%
17%–28%	96%	83%	95%	39%	70%	77%	44%	85%	56%	23%
Above 28%	94%	76%	91%	41%	67%	77%	47%	81%	65%	31%

*The percentages represented here and those represented in the collapsed categories in the report may differ slightly, due to the fact that the percentages represented in the report include those who did not respond to the question in the calculation of the percentage while the those represented above do not.

Appendix D

1996
Prior Learning Assessment Survey
Questionnaire

Current Practices in Prior Learning Assessment (PLA)

Name of
Institution:_____

Type of Institution: _____ public _____ private

Address of
Institution:_____

_____

City: _____ State:_____Zip: _____

Telephone: _____

Response Coordinator:_____

Title: _____

Address of Respondent: _____

_____

City:_____State:_____Zip:_____

Telephone: _____

If PLA is predominantly handled in one unit or college of the university and is not applicable to the whole
university, please indicate whether you are responding to the survey questions based on the unit or the
university as a whole:

_____ unit   _____ university (please check one)

Name of unit or
university:_____

_____

PLEASE DO NOT SUBSTITUTE YOUR COLLEGE POLICY MATERIAL OR BROCHURES IN LIEU OF
RESPONDING TO THESE QUESTIONS. THIS SURVEY IS BEING UTILIZED BECAUSE WE ARE
INTERESTED IN GATHERING COMPARABLE QUANTITATIVE INFORMATION FROM ALL SCHOOLS
THAT RESPOND TO THE SURVEY. IF YOU HAVE A BROCHURE ON PRIOR LEARNING ASSESSMENT
AT YOUR INSTITUTION, WE WELCOME THAT AS A SUPPLEMENT TO THIS QUESTIONNAIRE.
==
This space for office use only

Instructions for Completing the Questionnaire

The questionnaire is divided into three sections:

1. Prior Learning Assessment

A. Credit for Achievement on Advanced Placement Examinations (AP)

B. Credit for Appropriate Scores on the College Level Examination Program (CLEP) Exam

C. Credit for Appropriate Scores on the American College Testing Proficiency Examination Program

D. Credit for Appropriate Scores on Defense Activity for Non-Traditional Education Support (DANTES) Examinations

E. Course Challenge / Departmental Examinations

F. Credit Recommendations of the American Council on Education (ACE) Program on Non-Collegiate Sponsored Instruction (PONSI)

G. Credit Recommendations of the ACE GUIDE TO THE EVALUATION OF EDUCATIONAL EXPERIENCES IN THE ARMED SERVICES

H. Individual Prior Learning Assessment

I. Evaluation of Local Training Programs

2. Administration and Procedures for Prior Learning Assessment

3. Policy Governing Transfer of Awarded Prior Learning Assessment Credits from Other Institutions

Please complete all sections that apply to your institution

PRIOR LEARNING ASSESSMENT

	YES	NO

1. Does your institution assess prior learning for the award of credit through any national standardized exams, ACE recommendations or portfolio assessments? ☐ ☐

If no, please go directly to question number 1 on page 14.

2. If yes, can this credit be used to fulfill the requirements for:

	YES	NO
Associate's Degree?	☐	☐
Bachelor's Degree?	☐	☐
Major?	☐	☐
Minor?	☐	☐
General Education?	☐	☐
Master's Degree?		
Doctoral Degree?	☐	☐

3. Does a state policy group determine the number of credits that can be awarded through assessment? ☐ ☐

   If yes, please provide the name of the policy group(s):

_____

4. Does an accrediting body determine the number of credits that can be awarded through assessment? ☐ ☐

5. If yes, please provide the name of the accrediting body(s):

_____

Assessment Options

There are numerous nationally standardized exams and program assessments which have been conducted by national groups. All of the questions in Section II apply to these exams and programs. Please answer all that apply at your institution.

A. Prior Learning Assessment

	YES	NO
Credit for Achievement on Advanced Placement Examinations (AP)	☐	☐

1. Is credit for AP available at your institution? ☐ ☐
   If no, skip questions 2-9.

2. If yes, is there a level of proficiency or score required for credit awards? ☐ ☐

3. Is there a policy governing the award of AP credits? ☐ ☐

5. If yes, do the variations occur in:
_____ colleges   _____schools
_____ departments   _____divisions
_____ other programs

6. Is there an institution-wide policy governing the maximum number of credits that can be awarded for AP? ☐ ☐

7. If yes, please provide the maximum number that can be awarded: _____

8. Do policies regarding the maximum number of credits that can be awarded for AP vary across programs and majors? ☐ ☐

9. If yes, do the variations occur across:
_____colleges   _____schools
_____departments   _____programs
_____majors   _____other

B. Prior Learning Assessment   YES   NO
Credit for Appropriate Scores on
the College Level Examination
Program (CLEP) Exams

1. Does your institution award
credit for appropriate scores on
CLEP exams?   ☐   ☐
If no, skip questions 2-10.

2. If yes, is there a level of
proficiency or score required
for credit awards?   ☐   ☐

3. Is there an institution-wide
policy governing the award
of credit from CLEP exams?   ☐   ☐

4. Do policies regarding the
award of credit for CLEP
exams vary across academic
units?   ☐   ☐

5. If yes, do the variations occur in:
_____colleges   _____schools
_____departments   _____other programs

6. Is there an institution-wide
policy governing the maximum
number of credits that can be
awarded for CLEP exams?   ☐   ☐

7. If yes, please provide the maximum number
of credits that can be awarded:

_____

8. Do policies regarding the
maximum number of credits
that can be awarded for CLEP
exams vary across academic
units and/or programs
and majors?   ☐   ☐

9. If yes, do the variations occur in:
_____colleges   _____schools
_____departments   _____programs
_____majors   _____other

10. Can credits earned through
CLEP exams be used at both
the lower and upper division
level?   ☐   ☐

C. Prior Learning Assessment   YES   NO
Credit for Appropriate Scores
on the American College Testing
Proficiency Examination Program
(ACT-PEP) Tests

1. Does your institution award
credit for appropriate scores on
ACT-PEP tests?   ☐   ☐
If no, skip questions 2-10.

2. If yes, is there a level of
proficiency or score required
for credit award?   ☐   ☐

3. Is there an institution-wide
policy governing the awarding
of credit for ACT-PEP tests?   ☐   ☐

4. Do policies regarding the
award of credit for ACT-PEP
exams vary across academic
units?   ☐   ☐

5. If yes, do the variations occur in:
_____colleges   _____schools
_____departments   _____other programs

6. Is there an institution-wide
policy governing the maximum
number of credits that can be
awarded for ACT-PEP exams?   ☐   ☐

7. If yes, please provide the maximum number
of credits
that can be awarded: _____

8. Do policies regarding the
maximum number of credits that
can be awarded for ACT-PEP
vary across academic units
and/or programs and majors?   ☐   ☐

9. If yes, do the variations occur in:
_____colleges   _____schools
_____departments   _____programs
_____majors   _____other

10. Can credits earned through
ACT-PEP exams be used
at both the lower and upper
division level?   ☐   ☐

D. Prior Learning Assessment   YES   NO
Credit for Appropriate Scores on
Defense Activity for Non-Traditional
Education Support (DANTES)
Examinations

1. Does your institution award
credit for appropriate scores on
DANTES tests?   ☐   ☐
If no, skip questions 2-10.

2. If yes, is there a level of
proficiency or score required for
credit award?   ☐   ☐

3. Is there an institution-wide
policy governing the awarding
of credit for DANTES tests?   ☐   ☐

4. Do policies regarding the
award of credit for DANTES
exams vary across academic
units?   ☐   ☐

5. If yes, do the variations occur in:
_____colleges   _____schools
_____departments   _____other programs

6. Is there an institution-wide policy
governing the maximum number of
credits that can be awarded for
DANTES exam?   ☐   ☐

7. If yes, please provide the maximum number
of credits that can be awarded: _____

8. Do policies regarding the
maximum number of credits that
can be awarded for ACT-PEP
exams vary across academic
units and/or programs and majors? ☐   ☐

9. If yes, do the variations occur in:
_____colleges   _____schools
_____departments   _____programs
_____majors   _____other

10. Can credits earned through
DANTES exams be used at both
the lower and upper division level? ☐   ☐

E. Prior Learning Assessment   YES   NO
Course Challenge / Departmental
Examinations

1. Does your institution award credit
for Course Challenge examinations? ☐   ☐
If no, skip questions 2-11.

2. If yes, is the decision to give a Course
Challenge exam at the discretion of the:
_____colleges   _____schools
_____departments   _____programs
_____majors   _____instructors
_____other

3. If yes, is there a level of proficiency
or score required for credit awards? ☐   ☐

4. Is there a written policy
governing the award of credit
for Course Challenge exams?   ☐   ☐

5. Do policies regarding the award
of credit for Course Challenge
exams vary across academic units? ☐   ☐

6. If yes, do the variations occur because of:
_____colleges   _____schools
_____departments   _____instructors
_____other programs

7. Is there a written policy governing
the maximum number of
credits that can be awarded for
Course Challenge exams?   ☐   ☐

8. If yes, please provide the maximum number
of credits that can be awarded: _____

9. Do policies regarding the
maximum number of credits that
can be awarded for Course
Challenge exams vary across
academic units and/or programs
and majors?   ☐   ☐

10. If yes, do the variations occur because of:
_____colleges   _____schools
_____ departments   _____programs
_____majors   _____ instructors
_____ other

11. Can credits earned through Course Challenge exams be used at both the lower and upper division levels?　YES　NO　☐　☐

F. **Prior Learning Assessment**　YES　NO
Credit Recommendations of the American Council on Education (ACE) Program on Non- Collegiate (PONSI)

1. Does your institution award credit based on PONSI recommendations as they appear in the ACE guide without further review by faculty? If no, skip questions 2-11.　☐　☐

2. If yes, is there an institution-wide policy that governs the award of credit based on PONSI recommendations?　☐　☐

3. If no, do faculty or departments have a policy for reviewing the PONSI credit recommendations and awarding credit based on them?　☐　☐

4. Do policies regarding the utilization and acceptance of PONSI recommendations vary across academic units?　☐　☐

5. If yes, do variations occur in:
_____colleges　_____schools
_____departments　_____ other programs

6. Is there an institution-wide policy governing the maximum number of credits that can be awarded utilizing PONSI recommendations?　☐　☐

7. If yes, please provide the maximum number of credits that can be awarded:
_____

8. Do policies regarding the maximum number of credits which can be awarded based on PONSI recommendations vary across academic units and/or programs and majors?　☐　☐

If yes, what is the range of credits awarded?_____　YES　NO

9. If yes, do variations occur in:
_____colleges　_____schools
_____departments　_____programs
_____ majors　_____other

10. Can credits earned through PONSI recommendations be used at either the lower or the upper division level as recommended in the ACE guide?　☐　☐

At Master's level?　☐　☐

At Doctoral level?　☐　☐

11. If PONSI credit recommendations cannot be used at the graduate level, can they be used to help satisfy admission requirements?　☐　☐

G. **Prior Learning Assessment**　YES　NO
Credit Recommendations of the ACE GUIDE TO THE EVALUATION OF EDUCATIONAL EXPERIENCES IN THE ARMED FORCES

1. Does your institution award credit based on the credit recommendations in the ACE GUIDE TO EVALUATION OF EDUCATIONAL EXPERIENCES IN THE ARMED SERVICES? If no, skip questions 2-9.　☐　☐

2. If yes, is there an institution-wide policy governing the award of credit based on these ACE recommendations?　☐　☐

3. Do policies regarding the award of credit based on these recommendations vary across academic units?　☐　☐

4. If yes, do the variations occur in:
_____colleges　_____schools
_____departments　_____other programs

5. Is there an institution-wide policy governing the maximum number of credits that can be awarded based on these ACE recommendations? **YES NO** ☐ ☐

6. If yes, please provide the maximum number of credits that can be awarded based on these ACE recommendations?_____

7. Do policies regarding the maximum number of credits that can be awarded based on these ACE recommendations vary across academic units and/or program majors? ☐ ☐

8. If yes, do the variations occur in:
_____colleges _____ schools
_____ departments _____programs
_____ major _____ other

9. Can credits earned through these ACE recommendations be used at either the lower or the upper division level as recommended in the ACE guide? ☐ ☐

At the Master's level? ☐ ☐

At the Doctoral level? ☐ ☐

H. Prior Learning Assessment **YES NO**

Individualized Prior Learning Assessment

1. Does your institution award credit based on comprehensive assessment of prior learning from life and work experience by portfolio, oral interview, competence demonstration, or other procedures? ☐ ☐
 If no, skip questions 2-14.

At the undergraduate level? ☐ ☐

At the Master's level? ☐ ☐

At the Doctoral level? ☐ ☐

2. If yes, what methods of comprehensive assessment of prior learning are available for the award of credit? (Check all that apply) **YES NO**
_____portfolio
_____oral interview
_____course equivalencies
_____competence demonstration
_____other procedures

Please indicate other procedures:

_____

_____

3. Does your institution provide portfolio development courses or advising services for students who seek assessment of prior learning? ☐ ☐

If YES, please complete the following:

	Advising only	Course or Workshops	Credit Course	NO
a. Portfolio Assessment:	____	____	____	____
b. Oral Interview	____	____	____	____
c. Competence Demonstration	____	____	____	____
d. Other methods	____	____	____	____

If offered for credit, do students receive a grade for completion of the portfolio preparation course? ☐ ☐

If yes, is the grade (Please check):
_____numeric or letter?
_____pass or fail?
_____credit or no credit?

4. Is there an institution-wide policy governing the awarding of credit based on Comprehensive Assessment of Prior Learning? ☐ ☐

52

5. If yes, please provide the maximum number of credits/ competencies that can be awarded_____   YES   NO

6. Do policies regarding the award of credit based on Prior Learning Assessment vary across academic units?   ☐   ☐

7. If yes, do the variations occur in:
_____colleges   _____schools
_____departments   _____other programs

8. Do policies regarding the maximum number of credits that can be awarded based on the Assessment of Prior Learning vary across academic units and/or programs and majors?   ☐   ☐

9. If yes, do the variations occur in:
_____colleges   _____schools
_____departments   _____programs
_____majors   _____other

10. Can credits earned through assessment be applied at both the lower and upper division levels?   ☐   ☐

At Masters level?   ☐   ☐

At Doctoral level?   ☐   ☐

11. Is there a credit ceiling on the total number of credits accepted through all prior learning assessment options including testing, portfolio assessment, program evaluation, etc.   ☐   ☐

12. If yes, what is the ceiling?
_____

13. Does this ceiling vary across academic units?   ☐   ☐

14. If yes, do the variations occur in:
_____colleges   _____schools
_____departments   _____other

I. Prior Learning Assessment   YES   NO
Evaluation of Local Training Programs

1. Does your institution give standard credit awards for prior learning to students who possess a nationally recognized certificate of achievement (i.e. realtor's license, journeyman's card, LPM license)?   ☐   ☐

Please note specific certificates, licenses recognized:
_____
_____
_____

2. Are there other experientially based training programs for which your institution gives a standard award?   ☐   ☐

3. If yes, please indicate these programs:
_____
_____
_____

4. Do you utilize faculty teams to evaluate the training programs?   ☐   ☐

5. Has your institution been designated by your state higher education governing board to evaluate professional training programs for academic credit?   ☐   ☐

6. Does your institution use its own faculty to review training programs offered by local companies and make credit recommendations?   ☐   ☐

ADMINISTRATIONOF AND PROCEDURES FOR PRIOR LEARNING ASSESSMENT AT YOUR INSTITUTION
                                          YES   NO

1. Does your institution have a central office where students can find out about prior learning assessment procedures?   ☐   ☐

2. If yes, where is the office located?　　YES　NO
_____Registrar's Office
_____Admissions Office
_____Continuing or Adult Education Office
_____Other

3. How are these procedures publicized?

_____
_____
_____

4. Are there written guidelines on
what a student must prepare in
order to have his or her prior
learning assessed?　　☐　　☐

5. Is advisement and assistance
available to the student in preparing
the necessary materials?　　☐　　☐

6. Are credits awarded on the
basis of course equivalencies?　　☐　　☐

7. Does the student or the school determine the
credit request?
_____Student　　_____School

8. Is an interview with the
assessor a part of the
assessment procedure?　　☐　　☐

9. Is there an appeal procedure
for the student?　　☐　　☐

10. Is there a procedure which allows
the student to add additional
information for reassessment?　　☐　　☐

11. Who does the actual assessment of prior
learning?
_____Faculty in academic area of credit request
_____Specific faculty designated to perform
assessment
(without regard to area of request)

　Team of assessors composed of (check all
that apply):

_____faculty
_____counselor(s)
_____registrar
_____external experts

YES　　NO

Other administrative staff, please specify:

_____
_____
_____

Other, please specify:

_____
_____
_____

12. Do these same people make
the final credit recommendation?　　☐　　☐

13. If NO, who makes credit recommendations
(by title, not name of individuals)?

_____
_____
_____

14. Who receives these credit recommendations
and makes the award decisions?
(by title, not name of individuals)

_____
_____
_____

15. Is specific training provided
for the individuals who assess
prior learning and make
recommendations about
credit awards?　　☐　　☐

16. If YES, what is the nature of the training
they receive?

_____
_____
_____
_____
_____

17. If NO, would your institution
be interested in receiving training?　　☐　　☐

18. Do you have a faculty advisory
board to recommend
improvements in the portfolio
assessment program?　　☐　　☐

19. Is credit for prior learning shown on the student's transcript? (Please check those that apply)

    as credit:

                  _____with course title listed
                  _____without course title listed

    as credit:

                  _____with indication that credits

were earned through assessment?
                  _____with no indication that credits

were earned through assessment?
                  _____as a block of credits with

indication that credits were
earned through assessment?   ☐   ☐

20. When do you allow prior learning assessment to take place?
    (Please check those that apply)
    _____only prior to enrollment?
    _____at any time after enrollment?
    _____only after first year?
    _____both prior to and at any time after
        enrollment?

other, please indicate these restrictions:

_____
_____
_____
_____

21. Fee structure for assessment
    (check all that are applicable)

    _____tuition for the portfolio development
        courses
    _____evaluation fees
    _____posting fees
    _____other, please indicate:

22. Approximately how many students a year participate in the portfolio assessment program?

_____

23. What is the average number of credits that students earn through portfolio evaluation annually? _____

INSTITUTIONAL POLICY GOVERNING TRANSFER OF AWARDED PRIOR LEARNING ASSESSMENT CREDITS FROM OTHER INSTITUTIONS

                                  YES   NO

1. If another institution indicates on a transcript that credit was awarded for a course through assessment, do you accept the credit in transfer?   ☐   ☐

yes, but depends on
_____course area   _____academic unit
_____sending institution   _____other

2. If another institution indicates on a transcript that a block of credits has been awarded to a student through assessment, do you accept the credits in transfer?   ☐   ☐
    yes, but depends on:
    _____subject area
    _____academic unit
    _____sending institution
    _____other

3. Is the transfer of credits through assessment applicable to (Please check those that apply):

    _____lower division courses
    _____upper division courses
    _____master's level courses
    _____doctoral level courses
    _____all of the above

4. Is there a limit on the number of PLA credits accepted through transfer?   ☐   ☐

5. Is this policy set by your institution? ☐   ☐

6. Is this policy set by the university system?   ☐   ☐

7. Is this policy set by the state?   ☐   ☐

8. What is the institutional limit on transfer of credit through assessment?

_____

9. What is the designation assigned to transfer credits (Please check):

_____numeric or alphabetic
_____pass or fail
_____credit or no credit

10. If applicable, what is the state mandated limit on transfer credits earned through assessment?

_____

11. Does this limit differ from the acceptance of course credits in the transfer? ☐ ☐

12. Does your institution's policy regarding the acceptance in transfer of credits awarded through PLA differ from your institution's acceptance of other transfer credit? ☐ ☐

13. If yes, how?

_____
_____
_____

14. Is the transfer of credits through assessment applicable to (Please check those that apply):

_____major   _____minor
_____ general education requirements
_____electives   _____other
please indicate)

_____

PLA CONTACT

Who is the contact person at your institution for students interested in receiving more information about assessment of prior learning options at the undergraduate level?

Name: _____

Title: _____

Address:_____
_____

City: _____ State: _____ Zip:_____

Telephone:
_____

Who is the contact person at your institution for students interested in receiving more information about assessment of prior learning options at the graduate level?

Name: _____

Title:
_____

Address:_____
_____

City: _____ State: _____ Zip:_____

Telephone:
_____

Appendix E

1996
Prior Learning Assessment Survey
Participants

1996 Prior Learning Assessment Survey
[Recognition and Use of PLA by Institution]

AK

INSTITUTION	ANY PRIOR LEARNING ASSESSMENT	ADVANCED PLACEMENT	CLEP	ACT/PEP	DANTES	CHALLENGE EXAM	ACE/PONSI	ACE/MILITARY	INDIVIDUAL ASSESSMENT	ASSESSMENT OF CERTIFICATES
SHELDON JACKSON COLLEGE	X	X	X		X	X	X	X	X	
UNIVERSITY OF ALASKA ANCHORAGE	X	X	X	X	X	X	X	X	X	
AUBURN UNIVERSITY AT MONTGOMERY	X	X	X	X	X	X	X	X		

AL

INSTITUTION	ANY PRIOR LEARNING ASSESSMENT	ADVANCED PLACEMENT	CLEP	ACT/PEP	DANTES	CHALLENGE EXAM	ACE/PONSI	ACE/MILITARY	INDIVIDUAL ASSESSMENT	ASSESSMENT OF CERTIFICATES
AUBURN UNIVERSITY-MAIN CAMPUS	X	X	X			X				
BIRMINGHAM SOUTHERN COLLEGE	X	X	X			X			X	
FAULKNER UNIVERSITY	X	X	X		X		X	X		X
INTERNATIONAL BIBLE COLLEGE	X		X		X		X			
JEFFERSON DAVIS COMMUNITY COLLEGE-BREWTON CAMPUS	X	X				X		X		
JEFFERSON STATE COMMUNITY COLLEGE	X	X	X					X		
JOHN C. CALHOUN STATE COMMUNITY COLLEGE	X	X	X	X	X	X	X	X	X	X
LURLEEN B. WALLACE STATE JUNIOR COLLEGE	X	X	X			X		X		
MARION MILITARY INSTITUTE										
OAKWOOD COLLEGE	X	X	X		X	X		X	X	X
SOUTHERN CHRISTIAN UNIVERSITY	X				X		X	X		
SPRING HILL COLLEGE	X	X	X					X	X	
TROY STATE UNIVERSITY AT DOTHAN	X	X	X		X			X		

AL

INSTITUTION	ANY PRIOR LEARNING ASSESSMENT	ADVANCED PLACEMENT	CLEP	ACT/PEP	DANTES	CHALLENGE EXAM	ACE/ PONSI	ACE/ MILITARY	INDIVIDUAL ASSESSMENT	ASSESSMENT OF CERTIFICATES
TUSKEGEE UNIVERSITY	X	X	X					X		
UNIVERSITY OF MONTEVALLO	X	X	X			X		X		
UNIVERSITY OF NORTH ALABAMA	X	X	X		X			X		
UNIVERSITY OF SOUTH ALABAMA	X	X	X		X	X	X	X		
UNIVERSITY OF WEST ALABAMA	X	X	X	X	X			X		

AR

INSTITUTION	ANY PRIOR LEARNING ASSESSMENT	ADVANCED PLACEMENT	CLEP	ACT/PEP	DANTES	CHALLENGE EXAM	ACE/ PONSI	ACE/ MILITARY	INDIVIDUAL ASSESSMENT	ASSESSMENT OF CERTIFICATES
ARKANSAS STATE UNIVERSITY-MAIN CAMPUS	X	X	X	X	X	X	X	X		
ARKANSAS TECH UNIVERSITY	X	X	X	X		X		X		
GARLAND COUNTY COMMUNITY COLLEGE	X	X	X			X	X	X	X	
HENDRIX COLLEGE	X	X	X			X				
JOHN BROWN UNIVERSITY	X		X		X		X	X	X	X
MISSISSIPPI COUNTY COMMUNITY COLLEGE	X	X	X		X	X		X	X	X
NORTHWEST ARKANSAS COMMUNITY COLLEGE	X	X	X			X				
OZARKA TECHNICAL COLLEGE	X	X	X			X		X	X	
SHORTER COLLEGE										
SOUTHERN ARKANSAS UNIVERSITY-MAIN CAMPUS	X	X	X			X	X	X	X	
UNIVERSITY OF ARKANSAS AT MONTICELLO										
UNIVERSITY OF CENTRAL ARKANSAS	X	X	X		X	X		X		
WILLIAMS BAPTIST COLLEGE	X	X	X		X	X		X	X	

AZ

INSTITUTION	ANY PRIOR LEARNING ASSESSMENT	ADVANCED PLACEMENT	CLEP	ACT/PEP	DANTES	CHALLENGE EXAM	ACE/ PONSI	ACE/ MILITARY	INDIVIDUAL ASSESSMENT	ASSESSMENT OF CERTIFICATES
AMERICAN GRADUATE SCHOOL OF INTERNATIONAL MGMT	X		X		X					
CENTRAL ARIZONA COLLEGE	X	X	X			X		X		
GLENDALE COMMUNITY COLLEGE	X	X	X	X	X	X	X	X	X	X
MESA COMMUNITY COLLEGE	X	X	X	X	X	X	X	X	X	X
MOHAVE COMMUNITY COLLEGE	X		X		X	X		X		
NORTHERN ARIZONA UNIVERSITY	X	X	X	X	X	X			X	
PRESCOTT COLLEGE	X	X	X		X	X			X	
RIO SALADO COMMUNITY COLLEGE	X	X	X	X	X		X	X		X
UNIVERSITY OF PHOENIX-PHOENIX CAMPUS	X	X	X	X	X		X	X	X	X
YAVAPAI COLLEGE	X	X	X		X	X				X

CA

INSTITUTION	ANY PRIOR LEARNING ASSESSMENT	ADVANCED PLACEMENT	CLEP	ACT/PEP	DANTES	CHALLENGE EXAM	ACE/ PONSI	ACE/ MILITARY	INDIVIDUAL ASSESSMENT	ASSESSMENT OF CERTIFICATES
ALLAN HANCOCK COLLEGE	X	X	X		X	X		X		
ART INSTITUTE OF SOUTHERN CALIFORNIA	X					X		X		
AZUSA PACIFIC UNIVERSITY	X	X	X	X	X	X	X	X	X	
BETHANY COLLEGE OF THE ASSEMBLIES OF GOD	X	X	X		X	X		X	X	
BIOLA UNIVERSITY	X	X	X		X	X	X	X	X	
CALIFORNIA INSTITUTE OF INTEGRAL STUDIES	X	X	X		X		X	X	X	X
CALIFORNIA INSTITUTE OF TECHNOLOGY	X									
CALIFORNIA INSTITUTE OF THE ARTS	X	X								

INSTITUTION	ANY PRIOR LEARNING ASSESSMENT	ADVANCED PLACEMENT	CLEP	ACT/PEP	DANTES	CHALLENGE EXAM	ACE/PONSI	ACE/MILITARY	INDIVIDUAL ASSESSMENT	ASSESSMENT OF CERTIFICATES
CALIFORNIA LUTHERAN UNIVERSITY	X		X			X		X	X	
CALIFORNIA STATE UNIVERSITY-BAKERSFIELD	X	X	X		X	X		X	X	
CHAPMAN UNIVERSITY	X	X	X		X	X	X	X		X
CHRISTIAN HERITAGE COLLEGE	X	X	X	X	X		X	X	X	
CHURCH DIVINITY SCHOOL OF THE PACIFIC										
CLEVELAND CHIROPRACTIC COLLEGE OF LOS ANGELES										
COLLEGE OF NOTRE DAME	X	X	X	X	X	X	X	X		
CYPRESS COLLEGE										
GOLDEN GATE BAPTIST SEMINARY										
HEBREW UNION COLLEGE-CALIFORNIA BRANCH	X								X	
HOLY NAMES COLLEGE	X	X	X		X	X		X	X	
HUMBOLDT STATE UNIVERSITY	X	X	X			X		X	X	
LA SIERRA UNIVERSITY	X	X	X	X	X	X		X	X	
MENDOCINO COLLEGE	X	X				X	X	X		
MENLO COLLEGE	X	X	X		X		X	X	X	
MENNONITE BRETHREN BIBLICAL SEMINARY	X					X				
MOUNT SAINT MARY'S COLLEGE										
NATIONAL UNIVERSITY	X		X	X	X	X	X	X		X
NAVAL POSTGRADUATE SCHOOL										

INSTITUTION	ANY PRIOR LEARNING ASSESSMENT	ADVANCED PLACEMENT	CLEP	ACT/PEP	DANTES	CHALLENGE EXAM	ACE/ PONSI	ACE/ MILITARY	INDIVIDUAL ASSESSMENT	ASSESSMENT OF CERTIFICATES
NEW COLLEGE OF CALIFORNIA	X		X		X				X	
OTIS COLLEGE OF ART AND DESIGN										
PEPPERDINE UNIVERSITY	X	X	X			X	X	X		
PHILLIPS GRADUATE INSTITUTE										
PITZER COLLEGE	X	X							X	
SAINT JOHN'S SEMINARY COLLEGE	X	X								
SAINT MARY'S COLLEGE OF CALIFORNIA	X	X	X	X	X	X	X	X	X	
SAINT PATRICK'S SEMINARY										
SAN FRANCISCO THEOLOGICAL SEMINARY										
SAN JOSE CITY COLLEGE	X		X		X	X		X		
SANTA CLARA UNIVERSITY	X	X				X				
SAYBROOK INSTITUTE										
SCHOOL OF THEOLOGY AT CLAREMONT										
SCRIPPS COLLEGE	X	X	X							
SIMPSON COLLEGE	X	X	X		X	X				
SOUTHERN CALIFORNIA COLLEGE	X	X	X		X	X		X	X	X
SOUTHWESTERN UNIVERSITY-SCHOOL OF LAW										
STANFORD UNIVERSITY	X	X								
THE FIELDING INSTITUTE										

CA INSTITUTION	ANY PRIOR LEARNING ASSESSMENT	ADVANCED PLACEMENT	CLEP	ACT/PEP	DANTES	CHALLENGE EXAM	ACE/ PONSI	ACE/ MILITARY	INDIVIDUAL ASSESSMENT	ASSESSMENT OF CERTIFICATES
THE MASTERS COLLEGE	X	X	X					X	X	
THE UNIVERSITY OF WEST LOS ANGELES	X		X		X	X	X	X		
UNIVERSITY OF CALIFORNIA HASTINGS- COLLEGE OF LAW										
UNIVERSITY OF CALIFORNIA-DAVIS	X	X				X				
UNIVERSITY OF CALIFORNIA-LOS ANGELES	X	X						X		
UNIVERSITY OF CALIFORNIA-SANTA BARBARA	X	X								
UNIVERSITY OF JUDAISM	X					X				
UNIVERSITY OF LAVERNE	X	X	X	X	X	X	X	X	X	X
UNIVERSITY OF REDLANDS	X		X		X	X		X	X	X
UNIVERSITY OF SAN FRANCISCO	X	X	X		X	X	X	X	X	
UNIVERSITY OF SOUTHERN CALIFORNIA	X			X				X		
WEST HILLS COMMUNITY COLLEGE	X	X	X		X	X		X		
WESTMONT COLLEGE	X	X	X			X		X		
YUBA COLLEGE	X	X	X	X	X	X		X		

CO INSTITUTION	ANY PRIOR LEARNING ASSESSMENT	ADVANCED PLACEMENT	CLEP	ACT/PEP	DANTES	CHALLENGE EXAM	ACE/ PONSI	ACE/ MILITARY	INDIVIDUAL ASSESSMENT	ASSESSMENT OF CERTIFICATES
AIMS COMMUNITY COLLEGE	X	X	X	X	X	X	X	X	X	
COLORADO CHRISTIAN UNIVERSITY	X	X	X	X	X	X	X	X	X	X
COLORADO COLLEGE	X	X								
COLORADO SCHOOL OF MINES	X	X				X		X		

CO

INSTITUTION	ANY PRIOR LEARNING ASSESSMENT	ADVANCED PLACEMENT	CLEP	ACT/PEP	DANTES	CHALLENGE EXAM	ACE/PONSI	ACE/MILITARY	INDIVIDUAL ASSESSMENT	ASSESSMENT OF CERTIFICATES
DENVER CONSERVATIVE BAPTIST SEMINARY	X								X	
METROPOLITAN STATE COLLEGE OF DENVER	X	X	X	X	X	X	X	X	X	X
MORGAN COMMUNITY COLLEGE	X	X	X	X	X	X	X	X	X	
NAZARENE BIBLE COLLEGE	X		X			X		X		
REGIS UNIVERSITY	X	X	X	X	X	X	X	X	X	X
UNIVERSITY OF DENVER	X	X	X					X		
UNIVERSITY OF NORTHERN COLORADO	X	X	X		X	X		X		
WESTERN STATE COLLEGE-COLORADO	X	X	X		X		X	X		

CT

INSTITUTION	ANY PRIOR LEARNING ASSESSMENT	ADVANCED PLACEMENT	CLEP	ACT/PEP	DANTES	CHALLENGE EXAM	ACE/PONSI	ACE/MILITARY	INDIVIDUAL ASSESSMENT	ASSESSMENT OF CERTIFICATES
ALBERTUS MAGNUS COLLEGE	X		X	X	X	X	X	X	X	
BRIARWOOD COLLEGE	X		X	X		X			X	
CHARTER OAK STATE COLLEGE	X		X	X	X		X	X	X	X
CONNECTICUT COLLEGE	X	X						X		
HARTFORD SEMINARY	X								X	X
MANCHESTER COMMUNITY TECHNICAL COLLEGE	X		X		X	X		X		
NAUGATUCK VALLEY COMMUNITY-TECHNICAL COLLEGE	X	X	X			X			X	X
QUINNIPIAC COLLEGE	X	X	X			X	X		X	
SACRED HEART UNIVERSITY	X	X	X	X	X		X	X	X	

STATE	INSTITUTION	ANY PRIOR LEARNING ASSESSMENT	ADVANCED PLACEMENT	CLEP	ACT/PEP	DANTES	CHALLENGE EXAM	ACE/PONSI	ACE/MILITARY	INDIVIDUAL ASSESSMENT	ASSESSMENT OF CERTIFICATES
CT	THE HARTFORD GRADUATE CENTER										
	THREE RIVERS COMMUNITY-TECHNICAL COLLEGE	X		X		X	X	X	X	X	X
	TRINITY COLLEGE	X	X				X				
	UNITED STATES COAST GUARD ACADEMY										
	UNIVERSITY OF BRIDGEPORT	X	X	X			X			X	
	WESTERN CONNECTICUT STATE UNIVERSITY	X		X	X	X		X	X	X	
	YALE UNIVERSITY										
DC	BEAUFORT COUNTY COMMUNITY COLLEGE	X	X	X		X	X				
	CATHOLIC UNIVERSITY OF AMERICA	X	X	X							
	GALLAUDET UNIVERSITY	X	X	X							
	MOUNT VERNON COLLEGE	X	X	X		X	X		X	X	
DE	DELAWARE TECHNICAL AND COMMUNITY COLLEGE-TERRY	X		X		X	X		X	X	
FL	BARRY UNIVERSITY	X	X	X		X	X	X	X	X	X
	BETHUNE COOKMAN COLLEGE	X	X	X		X	X		X		

INSTITUTION	ANY PRIOR LEARNING ASSESSMENT	ADVANCED PLACEMENT	CLEP	ACT/PEP	DANTES	CHALLENGE EXAM	ACE/ PONSI	ACE/ MILITARY	INDIVIDUAL ASSESSMENT	ASSESSMENT OF CERTIFICATES
FL										
BREVARD COMMUNITY COLLEGE	X		X		X	X		X	X	X
CHIPOLA JUNIOR COLLEGE	X	X	X							
CLEARWATER CHRISTIAN COLLEGE	X	X	X					X		
EMBRY-RIDDLE AERONAUTICAL UNIVERSITY	X	X	X	X	X	X		X	X	
FLORIDA ATLANTIC UNIVERSITY	X	X	X	X	X					
FLORIDA BAPTIST THEOLOGICAL COLLEGE	X	X	X		X		X	X		
FLORIDA INSTITUTE OF TECHNOLOGY	X	X	X			X				
FLORIDA INTERNATIONAL UNIVERSITY	X	X	X		X			X		
FLORIDA KEYS COMMUNITY COLLEGE	X	X	X	X		X		X		
FLORIDA SOUTHERN COLLEGE	X		X		X		X	X		
FLORIDA STATE UNIVERSITY	X	X	X	X	X	X		X		
INTERNATIONAL COLLEGE	X	X	X	X	X	X	X	X	X	
LYNN UNIVERSITY	X	X	X	X	X	X	X	X	X	X
PALM BEACH ATLANTIC COLLEGE	X	X	X					X	X	X
PENSACOLA JUNIOR COLLEGE	X	X	X			X		X	X	
RINGLING SCHOOL OF ART AND DESIGN	X								X	
STETSON UNIVERSITY	X	X	X			X				
UNIVERSITY OF CENTRAL FLORIDA										
UNIVERSITY OF FLORIDA	X	X	X			X				

	INSTITUTION	ANY PRIOR LEARNING ASSESSMENT	ADVANCED PLACEMENT	CLEP	ACT/PEP	DANTES	CHALLENGE EXAM	ACE/PONSI	ACE/MILITARY	INDIVIDUAL ASSESSMENT	ASSESSMENT OF CERTIFICATES
FL	UNIVERSITY OF MIAMI	X	X	X		X					
	UNIVERSITY OF TAMPA	X	X	X	X	X	X	X	X	X	X
	WARNER SOUTHERN COLLEGE	X	X	X		X		X	X	X	X
	WEBBER COLLEGE	X	X	X		X			X		
GA	ABRAHAM BALDWIN AGRICULTURAL COLLEGE	X	X	X		X	X	X	X		
	AGNES SCOTT COLLEGE	X	X								
	ALBANY STATE COLLEGE	X	X	X		X	X		X		
	ANDREW COLLEGE	X	X	X		X	X		X	X	
	ARMSTRONG STATE COLLEGE	X	X	X	X	X			X		
	BRENAU UNIVERSITY	X	X	X	X	X	X		X	X	
	BREWTON-PARKER COLLEGE	X	X	X							
	BRUNSWICK COLLEGE	X	X	X		X			X	X	X
	CLARK ATLANTA UNIVERSITY	X	X	X							
	COLUMBIA THEOLOGICAL SEMINARY										
	COVENANT COLLEGE	X	X	X		X		X	X	X	
	EMMANUEL COLLEGE	X	X	X				X	X		
	GEORGIA INSTITUTE OF TECHNOLOGY- MAIN CAMPUS										
	GEORGIA STATE UNIVERSITY	X	X	X		X	X				

GA

INSTITUTION	ANY PRIOR LEARNING ASSESSMENT	ADVANCED PLACEMENT	CLEP	ACT/PEP	DANTES	CHALLENGE EXAM	ACE/PONSI	ACE/MILITARY	INDIVIDUAL ASSESSMENT	ASSESSMENT OF CERTIFICATES
MEDICAL COLLEGE OF GEORGIA	X		X	X		X			X	X
NORTH GEORGIA COLLEGE	X	X	X		X	X		X		
OGLETHORPE UNIVERSITY	X	X	X		X	X	X	X	X	
PIEDMONT COLLEGE	X	X	X		X			X	X	
REINHARDT COLLEGE	X	X	X							
SPELMAN COLLEGE	X	X	X						X	
TOCCOA FALLS COLLEGE	X	X	X		X		X	X		
TRUETT-MCCONNELL COLLEGE	X	X	X							
UNIVERSITY OF GEORGIA	X		X		X	X	X	X	X	
WESLEYAN COLLEGE	X	X	X			X	X	X	X	

HI

INSTITUTION	ANY PRIOR LEARNING ASSESSMENT	ADVANCED PLACEMENT	CLEP	ACT/PEP	DANTES	CHALLENGE EXAM	ACE/PONSI	ACE/MILITARY	INDIVIDUAL ASSESSMENT	ASSESSMENT OF CERTIFICATES
CHAMINADE UNIVERSITY OF HONOLULU	X	X	X		X	X		X	X	
HAWAII PACIFIC UNIVERSITY	X	X	X	X	X	X	X	X		X
LEEWARD COMMUNITY COLLEGE	X	X	X		X	X		X	X	
UNIVERSITY OF HAWAII AT WEST OAHU										

IA

INSTITUTION	ANY PRIOR LEARNING ASSESSMENT	ADVANCED PLACEMENT	CLEP	ACT/PEP	DANTES	CHALLENGE EXAM	ACE/PONSI	ACE/MILITARY	INDIVIDUAL ASSESSMENT	ASSESSMENT OF CERTIFICATES
BUENA VISTA UNIVERSITY	X	X	X		X		X	X	X	
CENTRAL COLLEGE	X		X	X	X	X	X	X		

INSTITUTION	ANY PRIOR LEARNING ASSESSMENT	ADVANCED PLACEMENT	CLEP	ACT/PEP	DANTES	CHALLENGE EXAM	ACE/ PONSI	ACE/ MILITARY	INDIVIDUAL ASSESSMENT	ASSESSMENT OF CERTIFICATES
CLARKE COLLEGE	X	X	X	X	X		X	X	X	
COE COLLEGE	X	X	X	X				X		
CORNELL COLLEGE	X	X	X			X				
DES MOINES COMMUNITY COLLEGE	X	X	X	X	X	X	X	X		
DIVINE WORD COLLEGE	X	X	X			X				
DORDT COLLEGE	X	X	X		X		X	X		
FAITH BAPTIST BIBLE COLLEGE AND SEMINARY	X	X	X			X		X	X	
GRACELAND COLLEGE	X	X	X	X	X	X	X	X	X	
GRINNELL COLLEGE	X	X								
INDIAN HILLS COMMUNITY COLLEGE	X	X	X		X	X				
IOWA LAKES COMMUNITY COLLEGE	X	X	X	X	X	X	X	X	X	X
IOWA STATE UNIVERSITY	X	X	X		X	X	X	X		
LORAS COLLEGE	X		X		X	X	X	X	X	
MAHARISHI UNIVERSITY OF MANAGEMENT	X	X	X	X	X			X	X	
MORNINGSIDE COLLEGE	X	X	X		X		X	X	X	
MOUNT MERCY COLLEGE	X	X	X	X	X			X	X	
MOUNT ST. CLARE COLLEGE	X	X	X			X		X		
NORTHWESTERN COLLEGE	X	X	X		X			X		
PALMER COLLEGE OF CHIROPRACTIC										

IA

INSTITUTION	ANY PRIOR LEARNING ASSESSMENT	ADVANCED PLACEMENT	CLEP	ACT/PEP	DANTES	CHALLENGE EXAM	ACE/ PONSI	ACE/ MILITARY	INDIVIDUAL ASSESSMENT	ASSESSMENT OF CERTIFICATES
SIMPSON COLLEGE	X	X	X		X	X		X	X	X
TEIKYO MARYCREST UNIVERSITY	X	X	X	X	X	X		X	X	
UNIVERSITY OF DUBUQUE	X	X	X	X	X	X		X	X	
UNIVERSITY OF IOWA	X	X	X	X		X	X	X		
WARTBURG COLLEGE	X	X	X			X	X	X	X	
WARTBURG THEOLOGICAL SEMINARY										
WESTMAR UNIVERSITY	X		X			X		X	X	X

ID

INSTITUTION	ANY PRIOR LEARNING ASSESSMENT	ADVANCED PLACEMENT	CLEP	ACT/PEP	DANTES	CHALLENGE EXAM	ACE/ PONSI	ACE/ MILITARY	INDIVIDUAL ASSESSMENT	ASSESSMENT OF CERTIFICATES
BOISE STATE UNIVERSITY	X	X	X	X	X	X	X	X	X	
LEWIS-CLARK STATE COLLEGE	X	X	X	X	X	X	X	X	X	
NORTHWEST NAZARENE COLLEGE	X	X	X			X				
RICKS COLLEGE	X	X	X			X				

IL

INSTITUTION	ANY PRIOR LEARNING ASSESSMENT	ADVANCED PLACEMENT	CLEP	ACT/PEP	DANTES	CHALLENGE EXAM	ACE/ PONSI	ACE/ MILITARY	INDIVIDUAL ASSESSMENT	ASSESSMENT OF CERTIFICATES
AUGUSTANA COLLEGE	X	X		X	X	X	X	X	X	
AURORA UNIVERSITY	X		X	X	X	X		X	X	
BARAT COLLEGE	X	X	X		X				X	
BELLEVILLE AREA COLLEGE	X	X	X		X			X	X	X
CARL SANDBURG COLLEGE	X	X	X	X	X			X		

INSTITUTION	ANY PRIOR LEARNING ASSESSMENT	ADVANCED PLACEMENT	CLEP	ACT/PEP	DANTES	CHALLENGE EXAM	ACE/ PONSI	ACE/ MILITARY	INDIVIDUAL ASSESSMENT	ASSESSMENT OF CERTIFICATES
CHICAGO THEOLOGICAL SEMINARY										
CITY COLLEGES OF CHICAGO-CENTRAL OFFICE	X	X	X	X	X				X	
COLLEGE OF SAINT FRANCIS	X	X	X			X	X	X	X	
COLUMBIA COLLEGE	X	X	X		X				X	
CONCORDIA UNIVERSITY	X	X	X	X	X	X	X	X	X	X
DEVRY INSTITUTE OF TECHNOLOGY	X		X		X	X		X		
DR. WILLIAM SCHOLL COLLEGE OF PODIATRIC										
ELMHURST COLLEGE	X	X	X					X	X	X
EUREKA COLLEGE	X	X	X		X					
GARRETT-EVANGELICAL THEOLOGICAL SEMINARY										
GOVERNORS STATE UNIVERSITY	X	X	X	X	X		X	X	X	
GREENVILLE COLLEGE	X	X	X		X	X	X	X	X	
HARRINGTON INSTITUTE OF INTERIOR DESIGN	X		X							
ILLINOIS BENEDICTINE COLLEGE	X	X	X	X					X	
ILLINOIS COLLEGE	X	X	X			X		X		
ILLINOIS COLLEGE OF OPTOMETRY										
ILLINOIS STATE UNIVERSITY	X		X		X			X	X	
ILLINOIS WESLEYAN UNIVERSITY	X	X	X							
JOHN WOOD COMMUNITY COLLEGE	X	X	X	X	X	X	X	X	X	X

INSTITUTION	ANY PRIOR LEARNING ASSESSMENT	ADVANCED PLACEMENT	CLEP	ACT/PEP	DANTES	CHALLENGE EXAM	ACE/ PONSI	ACE/ MILITARY	INDIVIDUAL ASSESSMENT	ASSESSMENT OF CERTIFICATES
JOLIET JUNIOR COLLEGE	X		X		X	X		X		
KANKAKEE COMMUNITY COLLEGE	X	X	X	X	X	X		X		
KENDALL COLLEGE	X	X	X	X	X	X	X	X	X	
KISHWAUKEE COLLEGE	X	X	X		X	X		X	X	
LAKE FOREST COLLEGE	X	X								
LAKE FOREST GRADUATE SCHOOL OF MANAGEMENT										
LEWIS UNIVERSITY	X	X	X		X	X	X	X	X	
LUTHERAN SCHOOL OF THEOLOGY AT CHICAGO	X					X				
MACCORMAC COLLEGE										
MACMURRAY COLLEGE	X	X	X		X		X	X		
MCCORMICK THEOLOGICAL SEMINARY	X								X	
MCKENDREE COLLEGE	X	X	X	X	X	X		X		
MENNONITE COLLEGE OF NURSING	X	X				X				
MONMOUTH COLLEGE	X	X						X		
MORAINE VALLEY COMMUNITY COLLEGE	X	X	X	X		X			X	X
NATIONAL-LOUIS UNIVERSITY	X	X	X	X	X	X	X	X	X	X
NORTH CENTRAL COLLEGE	X	X	X			X			X	
NORTH PARK COLLEGE AND THEOLOGICAL SEMINARY	X	X	X	X	X	X		X	X	
NORTHERN BAPTIST THEOLOGICAL SEMINARY										

INSTITUTION	ANY PRIOR LEARNING ASSESSMENT	ADVANCED PLACEMENT	CLEP	ACT/PEP	DANTES	CHALLENGE EXAM	ACE/PONSI	ACE/MILITARY	INDIVIDUAL ASSESSMENT	ASSESSMENT OF CERTIFICATES
NORTHWESTERN UNIVERSITY	X	X	X							
OLIVET NAZARENE UNIVERSITY	X	X	X	X	X	X	X	X	X	
PARKS COLLEGE OF SAINT LOUIS UNIVERSITY	X	X	X	X		X				X
QUINCY UNIVERSITY	X	X	X			X		X	X	
ROBERT MORRIS COLLEGE	X	X	X					X		
ROCKFORD COLLEGE	X		X					X		
ROOSEVELT UNIVERSITY	X	X	X		X	X		X		
ROSARY COLLEGE	X	X	X		X			X	X	
RUSH UNIVERSITY	X			X		X				
SAINT JOSEPH COLLEGE OF NURSING	X			X		X			X	
SAINT XAVIER UNIVERSITY	X	X	X	X	X	X	X	X	X	
SEABURY-WESTERN THEOLOGICAL SEMINARY										
TRINITY CHRISTIAN COLLEGE	X	X	X	X		X				
TRINITY EVANGELICAL DIVINITY SCHOOL	X		X			X		X		X
UNIVERSITY OF ILLINIOS AT SPRINGFIELD	X		X		X		X	X	X	
UNIVERSITY OF SAINT MARY OF THE LAKE										
WESTERN ILLINOIS UNIVERSITY	X		X	X	X	X		X	X	X
WHEATON COLLEGE	X	X	X			X		X		

IL

IN INSTITUTION	ANY PRIOR LEARNING ASSESSMENT	ADVANCED PLACEMENT	CLEP	ACT/PEP	DANTES	CHALLENGE EXAM	ACE/ PONSI	ACE/ MILITARY	INDIVIDUAL ASSESSMENT	ASSESSMENT OF CERTIFICATES
ANCILLA COLLEGE										
BETHEL COLLEGE	X	X	X	X	X	X	X	X	X	X
BUTLER UNIVERSITY	X	X	X	X	X			X		
CALUMET COLLEGE OF SAINT JOSEPH	X		X		X	X	X	X	X	
CHURCH OF GOD SCHOOL OF THEOLOGY										
CONCORDIA THEOLOGICAL SEMINARY										
DEPAUW UNIVERSITY	X	X							X	
EARLHAM COLLEGE	X	X								
FRANKLIN COLLEGE OF INDIANA	X	X	X		X			X		
GOSHEN COLLEGE	X	X	X		X	X	X	X	X	X
GRACE COLLEGE AND THEOLOGICAL SEMINARY	X	X	X	X	X	X	X	X	X	
HOLY CROSS COLLEGE	X	X	X							
HUNTINGTON COLLEGE	X	X	X	X	X		X	X	X	X
INDIANA INSTITUTE OF TECHNOLOGY	X		X		X		X	X	X	
INDIANA UNIVERSITY-BLOOMINGTON	X	X	X		X	X	X	X	X	X
INDIANA UNIVERSITY-EAST	X	X	X		X		X	X	X	
INDIANA UNIVERSITY-PURDUE UNIVERSITY-INDIANAPOLIS	X	X	X		X	X	X	X	X	X
INDIANA UNIVERSITY-SOUTH BEND	X	X	X		X	X	X	X	X	
IVY TECH STATE COLLEGE-CENTRAL INDIANA	X	X	X	X	X	X		X	X	X

IN

INSTITUTION	ANY PRIOR LEARNING ASSESSMENT	ADVANCED PLACEMENT	CLEP	ACT/PEP	DANTES	CHALLENGE EXAM	ACE/ PONSI	ACE/ MILITARY	INDIVIDUAL ASSESSMENT	ASSESSMENT OF CERTIFICATES
IVY TECH STATE COLLEGE-LAFAYETTE	X	X	X	X	X	X		X	X	
IVY TECH STATE COLLEGE-SOUTHWEST	X	X						X	X	
LUTHERAN COLLEGE OF HEALTH PROFESSIONS	X		X							
MANCHESTER COLLEGE	X	X								
MARTIN UNIVERSITY	X		X		X			X	X	X
PURDUE UNIVERSITY-CALUMET CAMPUS	X	X	X			X			X	
PURDUE UNIVERSITY-NORTHCENTRAL CAMPUS	X	X	X		X	X				
SAINT FRANCIS COLLEGE	X		X	X	X		X	X	X	
SAINT JOSEPHS COLLEGE	X	X	X				X	X	X	
SAINT MARY-OF-THE-WOODS COLLEGE	X	X	X	X	X	X	X	X	X	X
SAINT MARY'S COLLEGE	X	X	X							
SAINT MEINRAD COLLEGE	X	X	X					X		
TRI-STATE UNIVERSITY	X	X	X			X	X	X		
UNIVERSITY OF EVANSVILLE	X		X		X	X	X	X	X	
UNIVERSITY OF SOUTHERN INDIANA	X	X	X		X	X		X		X
VINCENNES UNIVERSITY	X	X	X	X	X	X	X	X	X	X
WABASH COLLEGE	X	X	X			X				

KS

INSTITUTION	ANY PRIOR LEARNING ASSESSMENT	ADVANCED PLACEMENT	CLEP	ACT/PEP	DANTES	CHALLENGE EXAM	ACE/ PONSI	ACE/ MILITARY	INDIVIDUAL ASSESSMENT	ASSESSMENT OF CERTIFICATES
BARCLAY COLLEGE	X	X	X	X	X			X	X	

KS

INSTITUTION	ANY PRIOR LEARNING ASSESSMENT	ADVANCED PLACEMENT	CLEP	ACT/PEP	DANTES	CHALLENGE EXAM	ACE/ PONSI	ACE/ MILITARY	INDIVIDUAL ASSESSMENT	ASSESSMENT OF CERTIFICATES
BARTON COUNTY COMMUNITY COLLEGE	X	X	X		X			X		
BENEDICTINE COLLEGE	X	X	X	X	X	X		X	X	
BETHEL COLLEGE	X	X	X			X		X	X	
BUTLER COUNTY COMMUNITY COLLEGE	X	X	X	X	X	X	X	X		X
CENTRAL BAPTIST THEOLOGICAL SEMINARY										
COLBY COMMUNITY COLLEGE	X		X			X		X	X	
DONNELLY COLLEGE	X	X	X			X			X	
EMPORIA STATE UNIVERSITY	X	X	X	X	X	X		X		
FORT HAYS STATE UNIVERSITY	X	X	X	X	X	X		X		
HESSTON COLLEGE	X		X			X		X		X
INDEPENDENCE COMMUNITY COLLEGE	X	X				X		X		
KANSAS NEWMAN COLLEGE	X	X	X	X	X	X	X	X	X	X
KANSAS STATE UNIVERSITY OF AGRICULTURE AND APP SCIENCE	X	X	X	X	X	X		X	X	
MANHATTAN CHRISTIAN COLLEGE	X		X	X	X	X	X	X	X	X
MIDAMERICA NAZARENE COLLEGE	X	X	X	X	X	X	X	X	X	
NEOSHO COUNTY COMMUNITY COLLEGE	X		X	X	X	X		X		
OTTAWA UNIVERSITY	X	X	X	X	X	X	X	X	X	X
PITTSBURG STATE UNIVERSITY	X	X	X		X	X		X		
SAINT LUKE'S COLLEGE										

KS

INSTITUTION	ANY PRIOR LEARNING ASSESSMENT	ADVANCED PLACEMENT	CLEP	ACT/PEP	DANTES	CHALLENGE EXAM	ACE/ PONSI	ACE/ MILITARY	INDIVIDUAL ASSESSMENT	ASSESSMENT OF CERTIFICATES
SAINT MARY COLLEGE	X	X	X	X	X	X	X	X	X	
SOUTHWESTERN COLLEGE										
TABOR COLLEGE	X	X	X	X	X	X	X	X	X	X
UNITED STATES ARMY COMMAND AND GENERAL STAFF COLLEGE										
UNIVERSITY OF KANSAS-MAIN CAMPUS	X	X	X		X	X		X		
WASHBURN UNIVERSITY OF TOPEKA	X		X			X		X		
WICHITA STATE UNIVERSITY	X	X	X		X	X		X	X	

KY

INSTITUTION	ANY PRIOR LEARNING ASSESSMENT	ADVANCED PLACEMENT	CLEP	ACT/PEP	DANTES	CHALLENGE EXAM	ACE/ PONSI	ACE/ MILITARY	INDIVIDUAL ASSESSMENT	ASSESSMENT OF CERTIFICATES
ASBURY THEOLOGICAL SEMINARY										
BELLARMINE COLLEGE	X	X	X	X	X	X	X	X	X	
BRESCIA COLLEGE	X	X	X			X	X	X	X	
CUMBERLAND COLLEGE	X	X	X		X	X		X		
GEORGETOWN COLLEGE	X	X	X							
LEXINGTON THEOLOGICAL SEMINARY										
LINDSEY WILSON COLLEGE	X	X	X		X	X		X		
LOUISVILLE PRESBYTERIAN THEOLOGICAL SEMINARY										
MADISONVILLE COMMUNITY COLLEGE	X	X	X	X		X	X	X		X
MAYSVILLE COMMUNITY COLLEGE	X	X	X	X	X	X	X	X	X	

KY

INSTITUTION	ANY PRIOR LEARNING ASSESSMENT	ADVANCED PLACEMENT	CLEP	ACT/PEP	DANTES	CHALLENGE EXAM	ACE/ PONSI	ACE/ MILITARY	INDIVIDUAL ASSESSMENT	ASSESSMENT OF CERTIFICATES
MURRAY STATE UNIVERSITY	X	X	X		X	X	X	X	X	
NORTHERN KENTUCKY UNIVERSITY	X	X	X			X	X	X	X	
OWENSBORO COMMUNITY COLLEGE	X	X	X	X	X	X	X	X		
PRESTONSBURG COMMUNITY COLLEGE	X	X	X	X	X	X	X	X	X	
SOUTHERN BAPTIST THEOLOGICAL SEMINARY	X		X			X				
SPALDING UNIVERSITY	X	X	X	X		X	X	X	X	
THOMAS MORE COLLEGE	X	X	X	X	X	X	X	X	X	X
UNION COLLEGE	X	X	X			X		X	X	
UNIVERSITY OF KENTUCKY	X	X	X		X	X	X	X		
WASHINGTON AND LEE UNIVERSITY	X	X				X				
WESTERN KENTUCKY UNIVERSITY	X	X	X	X	X	X				

LA

INSTITUTION	ANY PRIOR LEARNING ASSESSMENT	ADVANCED PLACEMENT	CLEP	ACT/PEP	DANTES	CHALLENGE EXAM	ACE/ PONSI	ACE/ MILITARY	INDIVIDUAL ASSESSMENT	ASSESSMENT OF CERTIFICATES
DELGADO COMMUNITY COLLEGE	X	X	X			X		X	X	
ELAINE P NUNEZ COMMUNITY COLLEGE	X	X	X		X	X		X	X	X
LOUISIANA COLLEGE	X		X			X		X		
LOUISIANA STATE UNIV & AGRL & MECH & HEBERT LAWS CT	X	X	X			X	X	X		
LOUISIANA STATE UNIVERSITY-ALEXANDRIA	X	X	X			X	X	X		
LOUISIANA STATE UNIVERSITY-EUNICE	X	X	X	X		X		X		X
MCNEESE STATE UNIVERSITY	X	X	X	X		X		X		

LA

INSTITUTION	ANY PRIOR LEARNING ASSESSMENT	ADVANCED PLACEMENT	CLEP	ACT/PEP	DANTES	CHALLENGE EXAM	ACE/PONSI	ACE/MILITARY	INDIVIDUAL ASSESSMENT	ASSESSMENT OF CERTIFICATES
NOTRE DAME SEMINARY GRADUATE SCHOOL OF THEOLOGY										
OUR LADY OF HOLY CROSS COLLEGE	X	X	X	X	X		X	X	X	
UNIVERSITY OF NEW ORLEANS	X	X	X			X	X	X		

MA

INSTITUTION	ANY PRIOR LEARNING ASSESSMENT	ADVANCED PLACEMENT	CLEP	ACT/PEP	DANTES	CHALLENGE EXAM	ACE/PONSI	ACE/MILITARY	INDIVIDUAL ASSESSMENT	ASSESSMENT OF CERTIFICATES
AMERICAN INTERNATIONAL COLLEGE										
AMHERST COLLEGE										
ASSUMPTION COLLEGE	X	X	X	X	X		X	X	X	
BAY PATH COLLEGE	X	X	X							
BENTLEY COLLEGE	X	X	X	X	X	X	X	X	X	
BERKSHIRE COMMUNITY COLLEGE	X		X		X	X	X	X	X	X
BOSTON COLLEGE	X	X								
BRADFORD COLLEGE	X	X	X		X		X	X		
BRIDGEWATER STATE COLLEGE	X	X	X		X	X		X		
BRISTOL COMMUNITY COLLEGE	X		X			X		X		
BUNKER HILL COMMUNITY COLLEGE	X	X	X	X	X	X	X	X	X	X
CAMBRIDGE COLLEGE	X		X	X	X	X	X	X	X	
COLLEGE OF OUR LADY OF THE ELMS	X	X	X		X	X		X	X	X
EMERSON COLLEGE	X	X	X							

MA

INSTITUTION	ANY PRIOR LEARNING ASSESSMENT	ADVANCED PLACEMENT	CLEP	ACT/PEP	DANTES	CHALLENGE EXAM	ACE/ PONSI	ACE/ MILITARY	INDIVIDUAL ASSESSMENT	ASSESSMENT OF CERTIFICATES
EMMANUEL COLLEGE	X	X	X	X	X	X	X	X	X	
FITCHBURG STATE COLLEGE	X	X	X	X	X	X	X	X		
GORDON COLLEGE										
GORDON-CONWELL THEOLOGICAL SEMINARY										
HELLENIC COLLEGE-HOLY CROSS GRK ORTH SCH OF THEOLOGY	X		X			X			X	
HOLYOKE COMMUNITY COLLEGE	X	X	X	X	X	X	X	X		X
LESLEY COLLEGE	X	X	X	X	X		X	X	X	X
MARIAN COURT COLLEGE	X					X			X	
MASSACHUSETTS MARITIME ACADEMY	X	X	X		X	X		X		
MASSACHUSETTS SCHOOL OF PROFESSIONAL PSYCHOLOGY										
MASSASOIT COMMUNITY COLLEGE	X	X	X	X	X	X	X	X	X	X
MOUNT HOLYOKE COLLEGE	X	X								
NEW ENGLAND COLLEGE OF OPTOMETRY										
NICHOLS COLLEGE	X	X	X	X	X	X	X	X		
NORTH SHORE COMMUNITY COLLEGE	X		X	X	X				X	X
NORTHEASTERN UNIVERSITY	X	X	X	X	X	X	X	X	X	X
PINE MANOR COLLEGE	X	X	X				X	X	X	
QUINSIGAMOND COMMUNITY COLLEGE	X	X	X	X	X	X	X	X	X	X
SAINT JOHN'S SEMINARY	X					X				

INSTITUTION	ANY PRIOR LEARNING ASSESSMENT	ADVANCED PLACEMENT	CLEP	ACT/PEP	DANTES	CHALLENGE EXAM	ACE/ PONSI	ACE/ MILITARY	INDIVIDUAL ASSESSMENT	ASSESSMENT OF CERTIFICATES
SALEM STATE COLLEGE	X	X	X	X			X	X	X	
SMITH COLLEGE	X	X								
SPRINGFIELD TECHNICAL COMMUNITY COLLEGE	X	X	X		X	X		X	X	
STONEHILL COLLEGE	X	X	X							
THE BOSTON CONSERVATORY	X	X	X	X	X		X	X	X	
UNIVERSITY OF MASSACHUSETTS-AMHERST	X	X	X	X	X	X	X	X	X	
WELLESLEY COLLEGE	X	X								
WENTWORTH INSTITUTE OF TECHNOLOGY	X	X	X			X		X	X	X

INSTITUTION	ANY PRIOR LEARNING ASSESSMENT	ADVANCED PLACEMENT	CLEP	ACT/PEP	DANTES	CHALLENGE EXAM	ACE/ PONSI	ACE/ MILITARY	INDIVIDUAL ASSESSMENT	ASSESSMENT OF CERTIFICATES
ANNE ARUNDEL COMMUNITY COLLEGE	X	X	X		X	X	X	X		
CAPITOL COLLEGE	X	X	X	X	X	X	X	X		
CECIL COMMUNITY COLLEGE	X	X	X	X	X	X		X	X	
COLLEGE OF NOTRE DAME-MARYLAND	X	X	X	X	X	X	X	X	X	
COLUMBIA UNION COLLEGE	X	X	X	X	X	X	X	X	X	X
DUNDALK COMMUNITY COLLEGE	X	X	X	X	X	X	X	X	X	X
GARRETT COMMUNITY COLLEGE	X	X	X	X	X	X		X	X	X
HARFORD COMMUNITY COLLEGE	X	X	X		X	X	X	X		
HOOD COLLEGE	X	X	X			X	X	X	X	
JOHNS HOPKINS UNIVERSITY	X									

MD

INSTITUTION	ANY PRIOR LEARNING ASSESSMENT	ADVANCED PLACEMENT	CLEP	ACT/PEP	DANTES	CHALLENGE EXAM	ACE/ PONSI	ACE/ MILITARY	INDIVIDUAL ASSESSMENT	ASSESSMENT OF CERTIFICATES
LOYOLA COLLEGE	X	X	X			X	X			
MISSOURI VALLEY COLLEGE	X	X	X	X	X		X	X		
MONTGOMERY COLLEGE-CENTRAL OFFICE	X	X	X	X	X	X		X	X	X
MORGAN STATE UNIVERSITY	X	X	X					X		
MOUNT SAINT MARYS COLLEGE	X	X	X		X		X	X	X	
SAINT MARY'S COLLEGE OF MARYLAND	X	X	X		X		X	X		
ST JOHN'S COLLEGE										
TOWSON STATE UNIVERSITY	X	X	X	X		X		X	X	
UNIVERSITY OF MARYLAND COLLEGE- PARK CAMPUS	X	X	X			X				
UNIVERSITY OF MARYLAND UNIVERSITY COLLEGE	X	X	X	X	X	X		X	X	
WASHINGTON COLLEGE	X									
WESTERN MARYLAND COLLEGE	X	X	X					X		

ME

INSTITUTION	ANY PRIOR LEARNING ASSESSMENT	ADVANCED PLACEMENT	CLEP	ACT/PEP	DANTES	CHALLENGE EXAM	ACE/ PONSI	ACE/ MILITARY	INDIVIDUAL ASSESSMENT	ASSESSMENT OF CERTIFICATES
COLBY COLLEGE										
MAINE MARITIME ACADEMY	X	X	X	X	X	X	X	X	X	
NORTHERN MAINE TECHNICAL COLLEGE	X	X	X	X	X	X		X	X	
SAINT JOSEPH'S COLLEGE	X	X	X	X	X	X	X	X	X	
THOMAS COLLEGE	X	X	X		X	X	X	X	X	

ME INSTITUTION	ANY PRIOR LEARNING ASSESSMENT	ADVANCED PLACEMENT	CLEP	ACT/PEP	DANTES	CHALLENGE EXAM	ACE/PONSI	ACE/MILITARY	INDIVIDUAL ASSESSMENT	ASSESSMENT OF CERTIFICATES
UNIVERSITY OF MAINE	X	X	X			X			X	
UNIVERSITY OF MAINE AT FARMINGTON	X	X	X		X	X		X		X
UNIVERSITY OF MAINE AT FORT KENT	X	X	X	X	X		X	X	X	
UNIVERSITY OF SOUTHERN MAINE	X	X	X		X	X	X	X	X	X

MI INSTITUTION	ANY PRIOR LEARNING ASSESSMENT	ADVANCED PLACEMENT	CLEP	ACT/PEP	DANTES	CHALLENGE EXAM	ACE/PONSI	ACE/MILITARY	INDIVIDUAL ASSESSMENT	ASSESSMENT OF CERTIFICATES
ALBION COLLEGE	X	X	X							
CALVIN COLLEGE	X		X		X			X	X	X
CENTER FOR CREATIVE STUDIES COLLEGE OF ART & DESIGN	X		X					X		
CENTER FOR HUMANISTIC STUDIES										
CENTRAL MICHIGAN UNIVERSITY	X	X	X	X			X	X	X	X
CONCORDIA COLLEGE	X	X	X	X		X	X	X	X	X
CORNERSTONE COLLEGE	X	X	X		X			X	X	X
DAVENPORT COLLEGE	X	X	X		X	X	X	X	X	X
DETROIT COLLEGE OF BUSINESS- DEARBORN	X	X	X	X	X	X	X	X	X	X
EASTERN MICHIGAN UNIVERSITY	X	X	X					X	X	X
FERRIS STATE UNIVERSITY	X	X	X		X	X		X	X	
GLEN OAKS COMMUNITY COLLEGE	X	X	X			X		X		
GMI ENGINEERING AND MANAGEMENT INSTITUTE	X	X				X				

INSTITUTION	ANY PRIOR LEARNING ASSESSMENT	ADVANCED PLACEMENT	CLEP	ACT/PEP	DANTES	CHALLENGE EXAM	ACE/ PONSI	ACE/ MILITARY	INDIVIDUAL ASSESSMENT	ASSESSMENT OF CERTIFICATES
GRAND RAPIDS COMMUNITY COLLEGE	X	X	X	X		X		X	X	X
GRAND VALLEY STATE UNIVERSITY	X	X	X					X		
GREAT LAKES JUNIOR COLLEGE OF BUSINESS	X							X		X
HILLSDALE COLLEGE	X	X	X							
KELLOGG COMMUNITY COLLEGE	X	X	X	X	X	X	X	X	X	X
KIRTLAND COMMUNITY COLLEGE	X	X	X		X			X		
LAKE MICHIGAN COLLEGE	X	X	X		X	X	X	X	X	
LAKE SUPERIOR STATE UNIVERSITY	X	X	X		X	X		X		
LANSING COMMUNITY COLLEGE	X	X	X		X	X		X	X	X
LAWRENCE TECHNOLOGICAL UNIVERSITY	X	X	X	X	X	X		X		
MADONNA UNIVERSITY	X	X	X			X	X	X	X	X
MICHIGAN CHRISTIAN COLLEGE	X	X	X		X	X	X	X	X	
MICHIGAN STATE UNIVERSITY	X	X	X			X				
MONROE COUNTY COMMUNITY COLLEGE										
MONTCALM COMMUNITY COLLEGE	X		X		X	X		X		
NORTHWESTERN MICHIGAN COLLEGE	X	X	X	X		X		X	X	
REFORMED BIBLE COLLEGE	X	X	X	X	X	X		X	X	
SAGINAW VALLEY STATE UNIVERSITY	X		X	X	X	X				
SAINT MARY'S COLLEGE	X	X	X		X	X	X		X	

MI

INSTITUTION	ANY PRIOR LEARNING ASSESSMENT	ADVANCED PLACEMENT	CLEP	ACT/PEP	DANTES	CHALLENGE EXAM	ACE/ PONSI	ACE/ MILITARY	INDIVIDUAL ASSESSMENT	ASSESSMENT OF CERTIFICATES
SCHOOLCRAFT COLLEGE	X	X	X		X	X		X		
SPRING ARBOR COLLEGE	X	X	X		X	X	X	X	X	X
ST. CLAIR COUNTY COMMUNITY COLLEGE	X	X	X			X			X	
THOMAS M. COOLEY LAW SCHOOL										
UNIVERSITY OF MISSOURI-KANSAS CITY	X	X	X	X		X		X		
WALSH COLLEGE OF ACCOUNTANCY AND BUSINESS ADMIN										
WAYNE STATE UNIVERSITY	X	X	X		X	X				
WESTERN MONTANA COLLEGE-UNIVERSITY OF MONTANA	X	X	X			X		X		

MN

INSTITUTION	ANY PRIOR LEARNING ASSESSMENT	ADVANCED PLACEMENT	CLEP	ACT/PEP	DANTES	CHALLENGE EXAM	ACE/ PONSI	ACE/ MILITARY	INDIVIDUAL ASSESSMENT	ASSESSMENT OF CERTIFICATES
ALFRED ADLER INSTITUTE OF MINNESOTA										
BETHANY LUTHERAN COLLEGE	X	X	X							
BETHEL COLLEGE	X	X	X	X	X	X	X	X	X	X
COLLEGE OF SAINT BENEDICT	X	X	X			X		X		
COLLEGE OF SAINT CATHERINE-SAINT CATHERINE CAMPUS	X	X	X	X			X	X	X	X
CONCORDIA COLLEGE	X	X	X	X	X	X	X	X	X	X
CONCORDIA COLLEGE AT MOORHEAD	X		X		X	X	X	X	X	X
GUSTAVUS ADOLPHUS COLLEGE	X	X				X				

INSTITUTION	ANY PRIOR LEARNING ASSESSMENT	ADVANCED PLACEMENT	CLEP	ACT/PEP	DANTES	CHALLENGE EXAM	ACE/ PONSI	ACE/ MILITARY	INDIVIDUAL ASSESSMENT	ASSESSMENT OF CERTIFICATES
HAMLINE UNIVERSITY	X	X	X		X	X		X		
LAKEWOOD COMMUNITY COLLEGE	X	X	X			X		X	X	X
LUTHER SEMINARY										
MACALESTER COLLEGE	X	X								
MANKATO STATE UNIVERSITY	X		X	X	X	X		X		
MARTIN LUTHER COLLEGE	X	X							X	
MINNESOTA BIBLE COLLEGE	X	X	X					X		
MOORHEAD STATE UNIVERSITY	X		X			X			X	X
NORMANDALE COMMUNITY COLLEGE	X	X	X		X	X		X	X	
NORTH CENTRAL BIBLE COLLEGE	X	X	X		X	X		X	X	
NORTHLAND COMMUNITY AND TECHNICAL COLLEGE	X	X	X		X			X		
NORTHWEST TECHNICAL COLLEGE-DETROIT LAKES	X		X	X	X	X	X	X	X	X
SAINT CLOUD TECHNICAL COLLEGE	X	X	X		X	X		X	X	
SAINT JOHN'S UNIVERSITY	X	X	X			X		X		
UNIVERSITY OF MINNESOTA-DULUTH	X	X	X					X		
UNIVERSITY OF MINNESOTA-TWIN CITIES	X	X	X	X	X	X		X	X	
WILLIAM MITCHELL COLLEGE OF LAW										

INSTITUTION	ANY PRIOR LEARNING ASSESSMENT	ADVANCED PLACEMENT	CLEP	ACT/PEP	DANTES	CHALLENGE EXAM	ACE/ PONSI	ACE/ MILITARY	INDIVIDUAL ASSESSMENT	ASSESSMENT OF CERTIFICATES
AQUINAS INSTITUTE OF THEOLOGY										

MO

INSTITUTION	ANY PRIOR LEARNING ASSESSMENT	ADVANCED PLACEMENT	CLEP	ACT/PEP	DANTES	CHALLENGE EXAM	ACE/ PONSI	ACE/ MILITARY	INDIVIDUAL ASSESSMENT	ASSESSMENT OF CERTIFICATES
CENTRAL METHODIST COLLEGE	X	X	X		X	X				
CENTRAL MISSOURI STATE UNIVERSITY	X	X	X			X		X	X	X
COLLEGE OF THE OZARKS	X	X	X			X		X		
COVENANT THEOLOGICAL SEMINARY	X					X				
CULVER-STOCKTON COLLEGE	X	X	X	X	X	X			X	
DEACONESS COLLEGE OF NURSING	X	X	X		X	X		X		
EAST CENTRAL COLLEGE	X	X	X			X		X		
EDEN THEOLOGICAL SEMINARY										
FONTBONNE COLLEGE	X	X	X			X	X	X	X	X
HANNIBAL-LAGRANGE COLLEGE	X		X	X	X	X		X	X	
HARRIS-STOWE STATE COLLEGE										
KENRICK GLENNON SEMINARY										
KIRKSVILLE COLLEGE OF OSTEOPATHIC MEDICINE										
LOGAN COLLEGE OF CHIROPRACTIC	X	X	X	X	X			X		
MIDWESTERN BAPTIST THEOLOGICAL SEMINARY										
MISSOURI SOUTHERN STATE COLLEGE	X	X	X			X		X		
NORTH CENTRAL MISSOURI COLLEGE	X		X		X	X	X	X		
PARK COLLEGE	X	X	X	X	X		X	X	X	X
ROCKHURST COLLEGE	X	X	X		X			X		

MO

INSTITUTION	ANY PRIOR LEARNING ASSESSMENT	ADVANCED PLACEMENT	CLEP	ACT/PEP	DANTES	CHALLENGE EXAM	ACE/ PONSI	ACE/ MILITARY	INDIVIDUAL ASSESSMENT	ASSESSMENT OF CERTIFICATES
SAINT LOUIS UNIVERSITY-MAIN CAMPUS	X	X	X	X	X	X		X	X	
SOUTHEAST MISSOURI STATE UNIVERSITY	X	X	X		X	X		X		
SOUTHWEST BAPTIST UNIVERSITY	X	X	X		X			X	X	
ST. CHARLES COUNTY COMMUNITY COLLEGE	X	X	X	X	X	X	X	X		
STEPHENS COLLEGE	X	X	X	X	X	X	X	X	X	
THREE RIVERS COMMUNITY COLLEGE	X	X	X					X		
WEBSTER UNIVERSITY	X	X	X	X	X		X	X	X	
WILLIAM JEWELL COLLEGE	X	X	X	X	X	X	X	X		
WILLIAM WOODS UNIVERSITY	X		X	X	X		X	X	X	

MS

INSTITUTION	ANY PRIOR LEARNING ASSESSMENT	ADVANCED PLACEMENT	CLEP	ACT/PEP	DANTES	CHALLENGE EXAM	ACE/ PONSI	ACE/ MILITARY	INDIVIDUAL ASSESSMENT	ASSESSMENT OF CERTIFICATES
BELHAVEN COLLEGE	X	X	X		X	X	X		X	
BLUE MOUNTAIN COLLEGE	X	X	X						X	
MISSISSIPPI COLLEGE	X	X	X			X		X		
MISSISSIPPI STATE UNIVERSITY	X	X	X			X		X		
MISSISSIPPI UNIVERSITY FOR WOMEN	X	X	X		X	X	X	X		
SOUTHWEST MISSISSIPPI COMMUNITY COLLEGE	X	X	X					X		

MT

INSTITUTION	ANY PRIOR LEARNING ASSESSMENT	ADVANCED PLACEMENT	CLEP	ACT/PEP	DANTES	CHALLENGE EXAM	ACE/ PONSI	ACE/ MILITARY	INDIVIDUAL ASSESSMENT	ASSESSMENT OF CERTIFICATES
CARROLL COLLEGE	X	X	X			X		X		

MT

INSTITUTION	ANY PRIOR LEARNING ASSESSMENT	ADVANCED PLACEMENT	CLEP	ACT/PEP	DANTES	CHALLENGE EXAM	ACE/PONSI	ACE/MILITARY	INDIVIDUAL ASSESSMENT	ASSESSMENT OF CERTIFICATES
DAWSON COMMUNITY COLLEGE	X	X	X		X	X		X	X	
DULL KNIFE MEMORIAL COLLEGE										
MONTANA STATE UNIVERSITY-BILLINGS	X	X	X	X	X	X	X	X		
MONTANA STATE UNIVERSITY-BOZEMAN	X	X	X			X		X		
MONTANA STATE UNIVERSITY-NORTHERN	X	X	X		X			X	X	
MONTANA TECH OF THE UNIVERSITY OF MONTANA	X	X	X		X	X	X	X		
ROCKY MOUNTAIN COLLEGE	X	X	X		X	X		X	X	X
STONE CHILD COLLEGE										
THE UNIVERSITY OF MONTANA-MISSOULA	X	X	X		X	X	X	X		

NC

INSTITUTION	ANY PRIOR LEARNING ASSESSMENT	ADVANCED PLACEMENT	CLEP	ACT/PEP	DANTES	CHALLENGE EXAM	ACE/PONSI	ACE/MILITARY	INDIVIDUAL ASSESSMENT	ASSESSMENT OF CERTIFICATES
CAMPBELL UNIVERSITY INC	X	X	X	X	X	X	X	X	X	
CARTERET COMMUNITY COLLEGE	X	X	X		X	X	X	X		X
CATAWBA COLLEGE	X	X				X		X		
CENTRAL CAROLINA COMMUNITY COLLEGE	X		X		X	X		X	X	
CHOWAN COLLEGE	X	X	X	X	X	X	X	X	X	
COASTAL CAROLINA COMMUNITY COLLEGE	X	X	X		X	X	X	X		
COLLEGE OF THE ALBEMARLE	X	X	X			X		X		
CRAVEN COMMUNITY COLLEGE	X	X	X		X	X		X		

NC

INSTITUTION	ANY PRIOR LEARNING ASSESSMENT	ADVANCED PLACEMENT	CLEP	ACT/PEP	DANTES	CHALLENGE EXAM	ACE/ PONSI	ACE/ MILITARY	INDIVIDUAL ASSESSMENT	ASSESSMENT OF CERTIFICATES
ELIZABETH CITY STATE UNIVERSITY	X	X	X					X		
FAYETTEVILLE TECHNICAL COMMUNITY COLLEGE	X	X	X	X	X	X	X	X		
GARDNER-WEBB UNIVERSITY	X	X	X	X	X	X		X		
GASTON COLLEGE	X	X	X			X		X		
GREENSBORO COLLEGE	X	X	X	X	X	X		X	X	
GUILFORD COLLEGE	X	X	X		X					
GUILFORD TECHNICAL COMMUNITY COLLEGE	X	X	X		X	X		X	X	X
HAYWOOD COMMUNITY COLLEGE	X							X		
HERITAGE BIBLE COLLEGE	X							X	X	
HIGH POINT UNIVERSITY	X	X	X		X	X	X	X	X	
JAMES SPRUNT COMMUNITY COLLEGE	X	X	X	X	X	X	X	X	X	
JOHN WESLEY COLLEGE	X		X		X	X	X	X	X	X
JOHNSON C. SMITH UNIVERSITY	X	X		X						
LENOIR-RHYNE COLLEGE	X	X	X	X	X	X	X	X		X
LOUISE HARKEY SCHOOL OF NURSING-CABARRUS MEM HOS	X	X	X			X			X	X
MARS HILL COLLEGE	X		X		X	X		X	X	
METHODIST COLLEGE	X	X	X		X	X		X		
NASH COMMUNITY COLLEGE	X		X					X		
NORTH CAROLINA CENTRAL UNIVERSITY	X		X		X	X		X		

NC

INSTITUTION	ANY PRIOR LEARNING ASSESSMENT	ADVANCED PLACEMENT	CLEP	ACT/PEP	DANTES	CHALLENGE EXAM	ACE/ PONSI	ACE/ MILITARY	INDIVIDUAL ASSESSMENT	ASSESSMENT OF CERTIFICATES
PEMBROKE STATE UNIVERSITY	X	X	X		X			X		
PFEIFFER COLLEGE	X	X	X		X	X	X	X	X	
PIEDMONT BIBLE COLLEGE	X		X							
PITT COMMUNITY COLLEGE	X		X			X		X		
RICHMOND COMMUNITY COLLEGE	X	X	X			X		X		
ROANOKE BIBLE COLLEGE	X	X	X	X	X			X		
ROANOKE-CHOWAN COMMUNITY COLLEGE	X		X		X	X		X		
ROBESON COMMUNITY COLLEGE	X	X	X		X	X		X		
SALEM COLLEGE	X	X	X					X	X	
SANDHILLS COMMUNITY COLLEGE	X	X	X		X	X			X	X
STANLY COMMUNITY COLLEGE										
SURRY COMMUNITY COLLEGE	X		X		X	X		X		
UNIVERSITY OF NORTH CAROLINA AT ASHEVILLE	X	X	X	X	X	X				
UNIVERSITY OF NORTH CAROLINA AT WILMINGTON	X	X	X					X		
WAKE TECHNICAL COMMUNITY COLLEGE	X		X		X	X			X	X
WESTERN CAROLINA UNIVERSITY	X	X	X		X	X	X	X	X	
WESTERN PIEDMONT COMMUNITY COLLEGE	X	X	X		X	X				
WILSON TECHNICAL COMMUNITY COLLEGE	X	X	X			X		X		X
WINGATE UNIVERSITY	X	X	X		X	X		X		

	INSTITUTION	ANY PRIOR LEARNING ASSESSMENT	ADVANCED PLACEMENT	CLEP	ACT/PEP	DANTES	CHALLENGE EXAM	ACE/PONSI	ACE/MILITARY	INDIVIDUAL ASSESSMENT	ASSESSMENT OF CERTIFICATES
NC	WINSTON-SALEM STATE UNIVERSITY	X		X	X	X	X	X	X		X
ND	DICKINSON STATE UNIVERSITY	X	X	X		X	X		X	X	
	JAMESTOWN COLLEGE	X	X	X	X	X	X		X	X	
	MEDCENTER ONE COLLEGE OF NURSING	X	X				X			X	
	NORTH DAKOTA STATE UNIVERSITY-MAIN CAMPUS	X	X	X		X	X	X	X	X	
	TRINITY BIBLE COLLEGE	X	X	X		X	X		X	X	
	UNIVERSITY OF MARY	X	X	X	X	X	X	X	X	X	X
	UNIVERSITY OF NORTH DAKOTA-MAIN CAMPUS	X	X	X	X	X	X		X	X	
	VALLEY CITYSTATE UNIVERSITY	X	X	X		X	X		X	X	
NE	CLARKSON COLLEGE	X	X	X				X	X		
	COLLEGE OF SAINT MARY	X		X	X	X	X	X	X	X	
	CREIGHTON UNIVERSITY	X	X	X	X	X	X		X	X	
	MIDLAND LUTHERAN COLLEGE	X	X	X	X	X	X	X	X		
	NEBRASKA WESLEYAN UNIVERSITY	X	X	X	X		X	X	X		
	NORTHEAST COMMUNITY COLLEGE	X	X	X		X		X	X		
	PERU STATE COLLEGE	X	X	X	X	X	X	X	X		

NE

INSTITUTION	ANY PRIOR LEARNING ASSESSMENT	ADVANCED PLACEMENT	CLEP	ACT/PEP	DANTES	CHALLENGE EXAM	ACE/PONSI	ACE/MILITARY	INDIVIDUAL ASSESSMENT	ASSESSMENT OF CERTIFICATES
UNION COLLEGE										
UNIVERSITY OF NEBRASKA AT KEARNEY	X		X			X	X	X	X	
UNIVERSITY OF NEBRASKA AT LINCOLN	X	X	X		X	X		X	X	
UNIVERSITY OF NEBRASKA MEDICAL CENTER	X	X	X		X	X		X		
WESTERN NEBRASKA COMMUNITY COLLEGE	X	X	X			X		X	X	
YORK COLLEGE	X	X	X		X	X		X	X	X

NH

INSTITUTION	ANY PRIOR LEARNING ASSESSMENT	ADVANCED PLACEMENT	CLEP	ACT/PEP	DANTES	CHALLENGE EXAM	ACE/PONSI	ACE/MILITARY	INDIVIDUAL ASSESSMENT	ASSESSMENT OF CERTIFICATES
COLLEGE FOR LIFELONG LEARNING	X	X	X	X				X	X	
DARTMOUTH COLLEGE	X	X								
FRANKLIN PIERCE COLLEGE	X	X	X		X		X	X	X	X
NEW ENGLAND COLLEGE	X	X	X		X		X	X	X	
NEW HAMPSHIRE TECHNICAL COLLEGE AT MANCHESTER	X	X	X	X		X	X	X	X	
NOTRE DAME COLLEGE	X	X	X		X	X	X	X	X	
PLYMOUTH STATE COLLEGE	X	X	X		X	X		X		
RIVIER COLLEGE	X	X	X	X	X	X	X	X	X	
UNIVERSITY OF NEW HAMPSHIRE-MAIN CAMPUS	X	X	X	X	X	X		X		

NJ

INSTITUTION	ANY PRIOR LEARNING ASSESSMENT	ADVANCED PLACEMENT	CLEP	ACT/PEP	DANTES	CHALLENGE EXAM	ACE/PONSI	ACE/MILITARY	INDIVIDUAL ASSESSMENT	ASSESSMENT OF CERTIFICATES
ASSUMPTION COLLEGE FOR SISTERS										

NJ

INSTITUTION	ANY PRIOR LEARNING ASSESSMENT	ADVANCED PLACEMENT	CLEP	ACT/PEP	DANTES	CHALLENGE EXAM	ACE/ PONSI	ACE/ MILITARY	INDIVIDUAL ASSESSMENT	ASSESSMENT OF CERTIFICATES
COLLEGE OF SAINT ELIZABETH	X	X	X	X	X			X	X	
GEORGIAN COURT COLLEGE	X	X	X		X		X	X		
MERCER COUNTY COMMUNITY COLLEGE	X	X	X	X	X	X		X	X	X
MIDDLESEX COUNTY COLLEGE	X	X	X	X	X			X		
MONTCLAIR STATE UNIVERSITY	X	X	X			X		X	X	
PRINCETON UNIVERSITY										
RAMAPO COLLEGE OF NEW JERSEY	X	X	X	X	X		X	X	X	
RARITAN VALLEY COMMUNITY COLLEGE	X	X	X		X	X	X	X	X	X
RUTGERS UNIVERSITY-NEW BRUNSWICK	X	X	X	X	X	X				
SALEM COMMUNITY COLLEGE	X		X		X	X	X	X	X	
THE RICHARD STOCKTON COLLEGE OF NEW JERSEY	X	X	X	X	X			X		
THOMAS A. EDISON STATE COLLEGE	X	X	X	X	X	X	X	X	X	X
TRENTON STATE COLLEGE	X	X	X		X	X		X		
UNION COUNTY COLLEGE	X		X		X	X				
WILLIAM PATERSON COLLEGE OF NEW JERSEY	X	X	X			X		X		

NM

INSTITUTION	ANY PRIOR LEARNING ASSESSMENT	ADVANCED PLACEMENT	CLEP	ACT/PEP	DANTES	CHALLENGE EXAM	ACE/ PONSI	ACE/ MILITARY	INDIVIDUAL ASSESSMENT	ASSESSMENT OF CERTIFICATES
COLLEGE OF SANTA FE	X	X	X	X	X	X	X	X	X	
COLLEGE OF THE SOUTHWEST	X	X	X	X	X	X	X	X	X	

INSTITUTION	ANY PRIOR LEARNING ASSESSMENT	ADVANCED PLACEMENT	CLEP	ACT/PEP	DANTES	CHALLENGE EXAM	ACE/PONSI	ACE/MILITARY	INDIVIDUAL ASSESSMENT	ASSESSMENT OF CERTIFICATES
NM										
NEW MEXICO JUNIOR COLLEGE	X	X	X			X		X		
NEW MEXICO MILITARY INSTITUTE	X	X	X		X	X	X	X		
SANTA FE COMMUNITY COLLEGE	X	X	X		X	X		X		
SOUTHWESTERN COLLEGE	X		X							
ST. JOHN'S COLLEGE										
WESTERN NEW MEXICO UNIVERSITY	X	X	X	X	X	X		X	X	
NV										
SIERRA NEVADA COLLEGE	X	X	X			X		X	X	
NY										
ALBANY LAW SCHOOL										
AMERICAN ACADEMY MCALISTER INST OF FUNERAL SERVICE										
BARNARD COLLEGE	X	X								
BROOME COMMUNITY COLLEGE	X	X	X			X			X	
CANISIUS COLLEGE	X	X	X	X	X	X			X	
CAYUGA COUNTY COMMUNITY COLLEGE	X	X	X		X	X	X	X		
CHRIST THE KING SEMINARY										
CLINTON COMMUNITY COLLEGE	X	X	X		X	X	X	X	X	
COLGATE UNIVERSITY	X	X	X							

NY INSTITUTION	ANY PRIOR LEARNING ASSESSMENT	ADVANCED PLACEMENT	CLEP	ACT/PEP	DANTES	CHALLENGE EXAM	ACE/PONSI	ACE/MILITARY	INDIVIDUAL ASSESSMENT	ASSESSMENT OF CERTIFICATES
COLLEGE OF MOUNT SAINT VINCENT	X		X		X	X		X		
COLLEGE OF NEW ROCHELLE	X		X						X	
COLLEGE OF SAINT ROSE	X	X	X						X	
CONCORDIA COLLEGE	X	X	X	X	X	X	X	X	X	
CROUSE IRVING MEMORIAL HOSPITAL SCHOOL OF NURSING	X	X	X						X	X
CUNY BROOKLYN COLLEGE	X	X	X	X	X	X		X	X	
CUNY COLLEGE OF STATEN ISLAND	X	X	X		X	X			X	
CUNY LA GUARDIA COMMUNITY COLLEGE	X	X		X	X	X	X	X	X	
CUNY LEHMAN COLLEGE	X	X	X	X	X	X	X	X	X	
D'YOUVILLE COLLEGE	X	X	X	X	X	X	X	X	X	
DAEMEN COLLEGE	X		X	X	X	X	X	X	X	
DOMINICAN COLLEGE OF BLAUVELT	X	X	X		X	X	X	X	X	
ERIE COMMUNITY COLLEGE-SOUTH CAMPUS	X		X	X	X	X		X	X	X
FINGER LAKES COMMUNITY COLLEGE	X	X	X		X	X	X	X		
FORDHAM UNIVERSITY	X	X	X						X	
FULTON-MONTGOMERY COMMUNITY COLLEGE	X	X	X	X	X	X	X	X	X	X
GENESEE COMMUNITY COLLEGE	X	X	X		X	X		X	X	X
HAMILTON COLLEGE	X	X								
HILBERT COLLEGE	X	X	X	X	X		X	X		

NY INSTITUTION	ANY PRIOR LEARNING ASSESSMENT	ADVANCED PLACEMENT	CLEP	ACT/PEP	DANTES	CHALLENGE EXAM	ACE/ PONSI	ACE/ MILITARY	INDIVIDUAL ASSESSMENT	ASSESSMENT OF CERTIFICATES
HOUGHTON COLLEGE	X	X	X	X	X	X	X	X	X	X
HUDSON VALLEY COMMUNITY COLLEGE	X	X	X	X	X	X	X	X	X	
INTERBORO INSTITUTE	X	X	X	X		X				
IONA COLLEGE	X	X	X			X	X	X	X	
ITHACA COLLEGE	X	X	X	X	X			X		
JEFFERSON COMMUNITY COLLEGE	X		X	X	X	X	X	X		
KEUKA COLLEGE	X	X	X	X	X	X	X	X	X	
MARIST COLLEGE	X	X	X	X	X			X	X	
MARYMOUNT COLLEGE	X	X	X						X	
MARYMOUNT MANHATTAN COLLEGE	X	X	X				X	X	X	
MOLLOY COLLEGE	X	X	X	X	X	X	X	X	X	X
MOUNT SAINT MARY COLLEGE	X	X	X	X	X	X	X	X	X	
MOUNT SINAI SCHOOL OF MEDICINE										
NASSAU COMMUNITY COLLEGE	X	X	X		X	X	X		X	X
NEW YORK INSTITUTE OF TECHNOLOGY-OLD WESTBURY	X	X	X	X	X	X	X	X	X	X
NEW YORK MEDICAL COLLEGE	X								X	
NIAGARA UNIVERSITY	X	X	X			X		X	X	X
PACE UNIVERSITY-NEW YORK	X	X	X	X	X	X	X	X	X	X
PAUL SMITH'S COLLEGE OF ARTS AND SCIENCES	X	X	X	X	X	X		X	X	

NY INSTITUTION	ANY PRIOR LEARNING ASSESSMENT	ADVANCED PLACEMENT	CLEP	ACT/PEP	DANTES	CHALLENGE EXAM	ACE/PONSI	ACE/MILITARY	INDIVIDUAL ASSESSMENT	ASSESSMENT OF CERTIFICATES
PRATT INSTITUTE-MAIN										
RENSSELAER POLYTECHNIC INSTITUTE	X	X						X		
ROBERTS WESLEYAN COLLEGE	X	X	X	X	X		X	X	X	X
ROCHESTER INSTITUTE OF TECHNOLOGY	X	X	X	X	X	X	X	X	X	
SAINT BONAVENTURE UNIVERSITY	X	X	X							
ST. FRANCIS COLLEGE	X	X	X	X	X		X	X	X	
ST. JOHN FISHER COLLEGE	X	X	X	X	X	X	X	X		
SAINT JOSEPH'S COLLEGE-MAIN CAMPUS	X	X	X		X		X	X	X	
SAINT JOSEPH'S SEMINARY AND COLLEGE										
ST. THOMAS AQUINAS COLLEGE	X	X	X		X		X	X	X	
SARAH LAWRENCE COLLEGE	X	X							X	
SCHENECTADY COUNTY COMMUNITY COLLEGE	X	X	X			X		X	X	
SEMINARY OF THE IMMACULATE CONCEPTION										
SIENA COLLEGE	X	X	X						X	
ST. JOSEPH'S HOSPITAL HEALTH CENTER SCHOOL OF NURSING	X	X	X		X	X				
ST. LAWRENCE UNIVERSITY	X	X	X	X						
SUFFOLK COUNTY COMMUNITY COLLEGE-AMMERMAN CAMPUS	X	X	X		X	X			X	
SUNY COLLEGE AT BROCKPORT	X	X	X	X		X	X	X	X	
SUNY COLLEGE AT GENESEO	X	X	X							

INSTITUTION	ANY PRIOR LEARNING ASSESSMENT	ADVANCED PLACEMENT	CLEP	ACT/PEP	DANTES	CHALLENGE EXAM	ACE/ PONSI	ACE/ MILITARY	INDIVIDUAL ASSESSMENT	ASSESSMENT OF CERTIFICATES
SUNY COLLEGE AT OLD WESTBURY	X	X	X		X				X	
SUNY COLLEGE AT POTSDAM	X	X	X		X		X	X		
SUNY COLLEGE AT PURCHASE	X	X	X				X	X	X	
SUNY COLLEGE OF AGRIC AND TECHN AT COBLESKILL	X	X	X			X	X	X		
SUNY COLLEGE OF ENVIRONMENTAL SCIENCE AND FOREST	X	X	X	X	X		X	X		
SUNY COLLEGE OF TECHNOLOGY AT ALFRED	X	X	X			X		X		X
SUNY HEALTH SCIENCE CENTER AT SYRACUSE	X	X	X	X		X		X		
SUNY MARITIME COLLEGE	X							X		X
SUNY ULSTER COUNTY COMMUNITY COLLEGE	X	X	X	X	X	X	X	X	X	
SUNY-SYSTEM OFFICE	X	X	X	X	X	X	X	X	X	X
SYRACUSE UNIVERSITY	X	X	X		X	X	X	X	X	
THE JUILLIARD SCHOOL										
TROCAIRE COLLEGE	X	X	X	X	X	X	X	X		X
UNITED STATES MERCHANT MARINE ACADEMY	X	X	X			X				
UTICA COLLEGE OF SYRACUSE UNIVERSITY	X	X	X	X	X	X	X	X	X	
VILLA MARIA COLLEGE-BUFFALO	X	X	X	X	X	X		X	X	
WELLS COLLEGE	X	X	X			X			X	

INSTITUTION	ANY PRIOR LEARNING ASSESSMENT	ADVANCED PLACEMENT	CLEP	ACT/PEP	DANTES	CHALLENGE EXAM	ACE/ PONSI	ACE/ MILITARY	INDIVIDUAL ASSESSMENT	ASSESSMENT OF CERTIFICATES
ASHLAND UNIVERSITY	X	X	X	X	X	X	X	X		
BALDWIN-WALLACE COLLEGE	X	X	X		X		X	X	X	
BLUFFTON COLLEGE	X	X	X	X	X	X	X	X	X	
BOWLING GREEN STATE UNIVERSITY- MAIN CAMPUS	X	X			X	X	X	X	X	
CAPITAL UNIVERSITY	X	X	X	X	X	X	X	X	X	X
CENTRAL OHIO TECHNICAL COLLEGE	X									
CLARK STATE COMMUNITY COLLEGE	X	X	X	X		X	X	X	X	
CLEVELAND COLLEGE OF JEWISH STUDIES										
CLEVELAND STATE UNIVERSITY	X	X	X		X	X	X	X	X	
COLLEGE OF WOOSTER	X	X						X		
COLUMBUS STATE COMMUNITY COLLEGE	X		X		X	X	X	X	X	X
DENISON UNIVERSITY	X	X								
FRANCISCAN UNIVERSITY OF STEUBENVILLE	X	X	X	X		X		X		
FRANKLIN UNIVERSITY	X	X	X	X	X	X	X	X	X	
GOD'S BIBLE SCHOOL AND COLLEGE	X		X							
HEBREW UNION COLLEGE-JEWISH INSTITUTE OF RELIGION										
HEIDELBERG COLLEGE	X	X	X	X	X	X	X	X	X	
HIRAM COLLEGE	X	X	X	X			X	X	X	
HOCKING TECHNICAL COLLEGE	X	X	X	X	X	X	X	X	X	X

INSTITUTION	ANY PRIOR LEARNING ASSESSMENT	ADVANCED PLACEMENT	CLEP	ACT/PEP	DANTES	CHALLENGE EXAM	ACE/ PONSI	ACE/ MILITARY	INDIVIDUAL ASSESSMENT	ASSESSMENT OF CERTIFICATES
KENT STATE UNIVERSITY-MAIN CAMPUS	X	X	X		X	X	X	X	X	
KENT STATE UNIVERSITY-STARK CAMPUS	X	X	X							
KENT STATE UNIVERSITY-TRUMBULL REGIONAL CAMPUS	X	X	X		X	X		X	X	X
KENYON COLLEGE	X	X								
LAKE ERIE COLLEGE	X	X	X		X		X	X	X	
LOURDES COLLEGE	X	X	X	X		X	X	X	X	X
MARIETTA COLLEGE	X	X	X		X	X	X	X	X	
METHODIST THEOLOGICAL SCHOOL-OHIO										
MIAMI UNIVERSITY-MIDDLETOWN	X	X	X			X		X		
MOUNT CARMEL COLLEGE OF NURSING										
MOUNT UNION COLLEGE	X	X	X						X	X
MOUNT VERNON NAZARENE COLLEGE	X	X	X			X		X	X	
MUSKINGUM COLLEGE	X	X	X	X		X	X	X	X	
NORTH CENTRAL TECHNICAL COLLEGE	X		X	X		X		X	X	X
NORTHWESTERN COLLEGE	X	X							X	
OHIO COLLEGE OF PODIATRIC MEDICINE	X								X	
OHIO DOMINICAN COLLEGE	X	X	X	X	X	X	X	X	X	
OHIO STATE UNIVERSITY-MAIN CAMPUS	X	X	X		X	X	X	X	X	
OHIO UNIVERSITY-EASTERN CAMPUS										

OH INSTITUTION	ANY PRIOR LEARNING ASSESSMENT	ADVANCED PLACEMENT	CLEP	ACT/PEP	DANTES	CHALLENGE EXAM	ACE/PONSI	ACE/MILITARY	INDIVIDUAL ASSESSMENT	ASSESSMENT OF CERTIFICATES
OHIO UNIVERSITY-MAIN CAMPUS	X	X	X			X		X	X	
OHIO WESLEYAN UNIVERSITY	X	X				X		X		
OWENS COMMUNITY COLLEGE	X	X	X			X		X	X	X
PONTIFICAL COLLEGE JOSEPHINUM										
SHAWNEE STATE UNIVERSITY	X	X	X	X	X	X		X		
SINCLAIR COMMUNITY COLLEGE	X	X	X		X	X	X	X	X	X
SOUTHERN STATE COMMUNITY COLLEGE	X	X	X	X	X	X	X	X	X	
THE UNION INSTITUTE	X	X	X	X	X	X		X	X	
TIFFIN UNIVERSITY	X	X	X	X	X	X	X	X	X	
TRINITY LUTHERAN SEMINARY										
UNITED THEOLOGICAL SEMINARY										
UNIVERSITY OF AKRON-MAIN CAMPUS	X	X	X		X	X		X	X	
UNIVERSITY OF CINCINNATI-MAIN CAMPUS	X	X	X	X		X			X	
UNIVERSITY OF DAYTON	X	X	X						X	
URSULINE COLLEGE	X	X	X			X		X	X	X
WALSH UNIVERSITY	X	X	X		X		X	X	X	
WASHINGTON STATE COMMUNITY COLLEGE	X	X	X			X		X	X	
WINEBRENNER THEOLOGICAL SEMINARY										
WITTENBERG UNIVERSITY	X	X	X			X				

OH

INSTITUTION	ANY PRIOR LEARNING ASSESSMENT	ADVANCED PLACEMENT	CLEP	ACT/PEP	DANTES	CHALLENGE EXAM	ACE/PONSI	ACE/MILITARY	INDIVIDUAL ASSESSMENT	ASSESSMENT OF CERTIFICATES
WRIGHT STATE UNIVERSITY-MAIN CAMPUS	X	X	X	X	X	X	X	X		
XAVIER UNIVERSITY	X	X	X	X			X	X		X

OK

INSTITUTION	ANY PRIOR LEARNING ASSESSMENT	ADVANCED PLACEMENT	CLEP	ACT/PEP	DANTES	CHALLENGE EXAM	ACE/PONSI	ACE/MILITARY	INDIVIDUAL ASSESSMENT	ASSESSMENT OF CERTIFICATES
BACONE COLLEGE	X	X	X			X		X		
CAMERON UNIVERSITY	X	X	X	X	X	X		X		
MURRAY STATE COLLEGE	X		X			X	X	X	X	
OKLAHOMA STATE UNIVERSITY-MAIN CAMPUS	X	X	X	X	X	X	X	X		
SOUTHERN NAZARENE UNIVERSITY	X	X	X		X	X	X	X	X	X
SOUTHWESTERN OKLAHOMA STATE UNIVERSITY	X	X	X		X	X	X	X		
UNIVERSITY OF TULSA	X	X	X	X		X				X
WESTERN OKLAHOMA STATE COLLEGE	X		X	X	X	X	X	X	X	X

OR

INSTITUTION	ANY PRIOR LEARNING ASSESSMENT	ADVANCED PLACEMENT	CLEP	ACT/PEP	DANTES	CHALLENGE EXAM	ACE/PONSI	ACE/MILITARY	INDIVIDUAL ASSESSMENT	ASSESSMENT OF CERTIFICATES
CHEMEKETA COMMUNITY COLLEGE	X	X	X			X		X	X	
CONCORDIA UNIVERSITY	X	X	X		X	X	X	X	X	X
EASTERN OREGON STATE COLLEGE	X	X	X			X		X	X	
EUGENE BIBLE COLLEGE	X		X					X	X	
LANE COMMUNITY COLLEGE	X	X	X		X	X	X	X	X	X
LEWIS AND CLARK COLLEGE										

INSTITUTION	ANY PRIOR LEARNING ASSESSMENT	ADVANCED PLACEMENT	CLEP	ACT/PEP	DANTES	CHALLENGE EXAM	ACE/PONSI	ACE/MILITARY	INDIVIDUAL ASSESSMENT	ASSESSMENT OF CERTIFICATES
LINFIELD COLLEGE	X	X	X		X	X	X	X	X	
LINN-BENTON COMMUNITY COLLEGE										
MARYLHURST COLLEGE	X	X	X	X	X	X	X	X	X	
MT. HOOD COMMUNITY COLLEGE	X	X	X			X		X	X	
NORTHWEST CHRISTIAN COLLEGE	X	X	X		X	X	X	X	X	
OREGON INSTITUTE OF TECHNOLOGY	X	X	X		X	X		X	X	
OREGON STATE UNIVERSITY										
PACIFIC NORTHWEST COLLEGE OF ART	X	X								
PACIFIC UNIVERSITY	X	X	X			X				
PORTLAND STATE UNIVERSITY	X	X	X		X	X		X		
SOUTHWESTERN OREGON COMMUNITY COLLEGE	X		X			X		X	X	
UMPQUA COMMUNITY COLLEGE	X	X	X	X	X	X	X	X		X
UNIVERSITY OF OREGON										
WARNER PACIFIC COLLEGE	X	X	X		X	X	X	X	X	X
WESTERN BAPTIST COLLEGE	X	X	X	X	X	X	X	X	X	
WESTERN CONSERVATIVE BAPTIST SEMINARY	X					X				
WESTERN OREGON STATE COLLEGE	X	X	X		X	X	X	X		
WESTERN STATES CHIROPRACTIC COLLEGE										

OR

PA

INSTITUTION	ANY PRIOR LEARNING ASSESSMENT	ADVANCED PLACEMENT	CLEP	ACT/PEP	DANTES	CHALLENGE EXAM	ACE/ PONSI	ACE/ MILITARY	INDIVIDUAL ASSESSMENT	ASSESSMENT OF CERTIFICATES
ALBRIGHT COLLEGE	X	X	X			X			X	
ALLENTOWN COLLEGE OF SAINT FRANCIS DE SALES	X	X	X		X	X		X	X	
ALVERNIA COLLEGE	X	X	X	X	X	X	X	X	X	
AMERICAN CONSERVATORY THEATER										
BAPTIST BIBLE COLLEGE AND SEMINARY	X		X		X	X	X	X	X	
BEAVER COLLEGE	X	X	X	X		X	X	X		
BIBLICAL THEOLOGICAL SEMINARY										
BLOOMSBURG UNIVERSITY OF PENNSYLVANIA	X	X	X			X		X	X	
BRYN MAWR COLLEGE	X	X								
BUCKNELL UNIVERSITY	X	X	X			X				
BUTLER COUNTY COMMUNITY COLLEGE	X	X	X	X	X	X	X	X	X	
CABRINI COLLEGE	X	X	X	X	X	X	X	X	X	X
CARLOW COLLEGE	X	X	X	X		X	X	X	X	
CARNEGIE MELLON UNIVERSITY										
CHESTNUT HILL COLLEGE	X	X	X			X				
COLLEGE MISERICORDIA	X	X	X	X				X	X	
DELAWARE COUNTY COMMUNITY COLLEGE	X	X	X	X	X	X		X	X	X
DELAWARE VALLEY COLLEGE	X	X	X			X		X		
DICKINSON COLLEGE	X	X								

INSTITUTION	ANY PRIOR LEARNING ASSESSMENT	ADVANCED PLACEMENT	CLEP	ACT/PEP	DANTES	CHALLENGE EXAM	ACE/PONSI	ACE/MILITARY	INDIVIDUAL ASSESSMENT	ASSESSMENT OF CERTIFICATES
DREXEL UNIVERSITY	X		X			X			X	
EAST STROUDSBURG UNIVERSITY OF PENNSYLVANIA	X	X	X			X				
EASTERN COLLEGE	X	X	X	X	X		X	X	X	X
EDINBORO UNIVERSITY OF PENNSYLVANIA	X	X	X	X		X		X	X	X
ELIZABETHTOWN COLLEGE	X		X		X	X	X	X	X	
FRANKLIN AND MARSHALL COLLEGE	X		X			X				
GENEVA COLLEGE	X	X	X	X	X	X	X	X	X	X
GWYNEDD-MERCY COLLEGE	X	X	X	X	X	X		X	X	X
HARRISBURG AREA COMMUNITY COLLEGE-HARRISBURG	X	X	X	X		X		X	X	X
HAVERFORD COLLEGE	X	X								
HOLY FAMILY COLLEGE	X	X	X		X	X	X	X		
IMMACULATA COLLEGE	X	X	X	X	X	X	X	X	X	X
KEYSTONE COLLEGE	X		X			X		X		X
KING'S COLLEGE	X	X	X	X				X		
LA ROCHE COLLEGE	X	X	X	X	X	X	X	X	X	X
LA SALLE UNIVERSITY	X	X	X	X	X	X	X	X		
LACKAWANNA JUNIOR COLLEGE	X	X	X		X	X	X	X	X	X
LAFAYETTE COLLEGE										
LANCASTER BIBLE COLLEGE	X	X	X		X		X	X	X	X

INSTITUTION	ANY PRIOR LEARNING ASSESSMENT	ADVANCED PLACEMENT	CLEP	ACT/PEP	DANTES	CHALLENGE EXAM	ACE/ PONSI	ACE/ MILITARY	INDIVIDUAL ASSESSMENT	ASSESSMENT OF CERTIFICATES
LEBANON VALLEY COLLEGE	X		X	X	X	X	X	X	X	
LINCOLN UNIVERSITY										
LUTHERAN THEOLOGICAL SEMINARY AT GETTYSBURG	X					X				
LUTHERAN THEOLOGICAL SEMINARY AT PHILADELPHIA										
LYCOMING COLLEGE	X	X	X	X	X	X				
MARYWOOD COLLEGE	X	X	X	X	X	X	X	X	X	
MORAVIAN COLLEGE	X	X	X		X	X				
MOUNT ALOYSIUS COLLEGE	X	X	X	X		X			X	
MUHLENBERG COLLEGE	X		X		X		X		X	
NEUMANN COLLEGE	X	X	X	X	X	X	X	X	X	
NORTHAMPTON COUNTY AREA COMMUNITY COLLEGE	X	X	X	X	X	X	X	X		
PEIRCE COLLEGE	X	X	X		X	X		X		
PENNSYLVANIA COLLEGE OF PODIATRIC MEDICINE	X					X				
PENNSYLVANIA INSTITUTE OF TECHNOLOGY	X		X		X	X		X	X	X
PENNSYLVANIA STATE UNIVERSITY-CENTRAL OFFICE	X	X	X		X	X		X	X	
PHILADELPHIA COLLEGE OF BIBLE	X	X	X					X	X	
PITTSBURGH THEOLOGICAL SEMINARY										
POINT PARK COLLEGE	X	X	X		X	X	X	X	X	X
READING AREA COMMUNITY COLLEGE	X	X	X	X		X			X	

PA

INSTITUTION	ANY PRIOR LEARNING ASSESSMENT	ADVANCED PLACEMENT	CLEP	ACT/PEP	DANTES	CHALLENGE EXAM	ACE/PONSI	ACE/MILITARY	INDIVIDUAL ASSESSMENT	ASSESSMENT OF CERTIFICATES
ROBERT MORRIS COLLEGE	X		X	X	X	X		X		
ROSEMONT COLLEGE	X	X	X		X		X	X	X	
SAINT JOSEPH'S UNIVERSITY	X	X				X				
SAINT VINCENT COLLEGE	X	X	X		X	X		X	X	
SLIPPERY ROCK UNIVERSITY OF PENNSYLVANIA	X	X	X	X	X	X		X		
SUSQUEHANNA UNIVERSITY	X		X						X	
SWARTHMORE COLLEGE	X	X								
TEMPLE UNIVERSITY	X	X	X							
THIEL COLLEGE	X	X	X	X	X	X		X	X	
UNIVERSITY OF SCRANTON	X		X	X	X	X	X	X	X	X
VALLEY FORGE MILITARY COLLEGE	X	X	X		X		X	X		
VILLANOVA UNIVERSITY	X	X	X	X		X				
WASHINGTON AND JEFFERSON COLLEGE	X	X	X					X		
WAYNESBURG COLLEGE	X		X	X	X	X	X	X	X	
WESTMINSTER THEOLOGICAL SEMINARY										
WIDENER UNIVERSITY-MAIN CAMPUS	X	X	X		X	X	X	X	X	
YORK COLLEGE-PENNSYLVANIA	X	X	X	X	X	X	X	X		

RI

INSTITUTION	ANY PRIOR LEARNING ASSESSMENT	ADVANCED PLACEMENT	CLEP	ACT/PEP	DANTES	CHALLENGE EXAM	ACE/PONSI	ACE/MILITARY	INDIVIDUAL ASSESSMENT	ASSESSMENT OF CERTIFICATES
NEW ENGLAND INSTITUTE OF TECHNOLOGY	X		X		X	X	X	X	X	X

SC

INSTITUTION	ANY PRIOR LEARNING ASSESSMENT	ADVANCED PLACEMENT	CLEP	ACT/PEP	DANTES	CHALLENGE EXAM	ACE/PONSI	ACE/MILITARY	INDIVIDUAL ASSESSMENT	ASSESSMENT OF CERTIFICATES
AIKEN TECHNICAL COLLEGE	X	X	X			X		X		
CLEMSON UNIVERSITY	X					X				
COKER COLLEGE	X	X	X		X	X	X	X	X	
COLUMBIA COLLEGE	X	X	X			X			X	
COLUMBIA INTERNATIONAL UNIVERSITY	X	X	X		X			X		
COLUMBIA JUNIOR COLLEGE OF BUSINESS										
CONVERSE COLLEGE	X	X				X			X	
FURMAN UNIVERSITY	X	X				X				
GREENVILLE TECHNICAL COLLEGE	X	X	X		X	X		X		
HORRY-GEORGETOWN TECHNICAL COLLEGE	X	X	X			X	X	X	X	
LIMESTONE COLLEGE	X	X	X		X	X	X	X		
NEWBERRY COLLEGE	X	X	X		X			X		
SPARTANBURG METHODIST COLLEGE	X	X	X							
TRI-COUNTY TECHNICAL COLLEGE	X	X	X	X	X	X		X	X	X
UNIVERSITY OF SOUTH CAROLINA AT SPARTANBURG	X	X	X	X	X	X		X		
WOFFORD COLLEGE	X	X	X		X			X		

SD

INSTITUTION	ANY PRIOR LEARNING ASSESSMENT	ADVANCED PLACEMENT	CLEP	ACT/PEP	DANTES	CHALLENGE EXAM	ACE/PONSI	ACE/MILITARY	INDIVIDUAL ASSESSMENT	ASSESSMENT OF CERTIFICATES
AUGUSTANA COLLEGE	X	X	X	X	X	X		X	X	
DAKOTA STATE UNIVERSITY	X	X	X		X	X	X	X	X	

SD

INSTITUTION	ANY PRIOR LEARNING ASSESSMENT	ADVANCED PLACEMENT	CLEP	ACT/PEP	DANTES	CHALLENGE EXAM	ACE/ PONSI	ACE/ MILITARY	INDIVIDUAL ASSESSMENT	ASSESSMENT OF CERTIFICATES
HURON UNIVERSITY	X	X	X	X	X	X		X	X	
NATIONAL COLLEGE	X		X	X	X	X	X	X	X	X
NORTHERN STATE UNIVERSITY	X	X	X		X	X	X	X		
PRESENTATION COLLEGE	X		X	X		X			X	
SINTE GLESKA UNIVERSITY	X					X				
SOUTH DAKOTA SCHOOL OF MINES AND TECHNOLOGY	X	X	X			X		X		
SOUTH DAKOTA STATE UNIVERSITY	X	X	X	X	X	X				
UNIVERSITY OF SIOUX FALLS	X	X	X		X	X	X	X	X	
UNIVERSITY OF SOUTH DAKOTA	X	X	X		X	X		X		

TN

INSTITUTION	ANY PRIOR LEARNING ASSESSMENT	ADVANCED PLACEMENT	CLEP	ACT/PEP	DANTES	CHALLENGE EXAM	ACE/ PONSI	ACE/ MILITARY	INDIVIDUAL ASSESSMENT	ASSESSMENT OF CERTIFICATES
AQUINAS COLLEGE	X	X								
AUSTIN PEAY STATE UNIVERSITY	X	X	X	X	X	X	X	X		
BELMONT UNIVERSITY	X	X	X		X	X	X	X		
BETHEL COLLEGE	X	X	X		X		X	X	X	
CARSON-NEWMAN COLLEGE	X	X	X	X	X	X		X	X	
CLEVELAND STATE COMMUNITY COLLEGE	X	X	X		X	X		X	X	X
CUMBERLAND UNIVERSITY	X	X	X	X	X		X	X	X	
DRAUGHONS JUNIOR COLLEGE OF BUSINESS										

TN

INSTITUTION	ANY PRIOR LEARNING ASSESSMENT	ADVANCED PLACEMENT	CLEP	ACT/PEP	DANTES	CHALLENGE EXAM	ACE/ PONSI	ACE/ MILITARY	INDIVIDUAL ASSESSMENT	ASSESSMENT OF CERTIFICATES
EAST TENNESSEE STATE UNIVERSITY	X	X	X	X	X	X	X	X	X	
FREED-HARDEMAN UNIVERSITY	X	X	X		X	X		X		
KING COLLEGE	X	X	X					X		
LAMBUTH UNIVERSITY	X	X	X	X	X		X	X		
LANE COLLEGE	X	X	X							
LEE COLLEGE	X	X	X		X	X		X		
LINCOLN MEMORIAL UNIVERSITY	X	X	X			X		X	X	
MEHARRY MEDICAL COLLEGE	X	X	X	X	X	X		X		
MEMPHIS THEOLOGICAL SEMINARY										
MID-AMERICA BAPTIST SEMINARY										
MILLIGAN COLLEGE	X	X	X	X	X		X	X	X	X
RHODES COLLEGE										
SOUTHERN COLLEGE OF SEVENTH-DAY ADVENTISTS	X	X	X			X		X		
STATE TECHNICAL INSTITUTE AT MEMPHIS	X	X	X		X	X		X	X	X
TENNESSEE WESLEYAN COLLEGE	X	X	X		X	X	X	X		
TREVECCA NAZARENE COLLEGE	X	X	X	X	X		X	X	X	X
TUSCULUM COLLEGE	X	X	X	X			X	X	X	
UNIVERSITY OF TENNESSEE-CHATTANOOGA	X	X	X	X		X		X	X	
UNIVERSITY OF TENNESSEE-KNOXVILLE	X	X	X		X	X		X		

TN INSTITUTION	ANY PRIOR LEARNING ASSESSMENT	ADVANCED PLACEMENT	CLEP	ACT/PEP	DANTES	CHALLENGE EXAM	ACE/ PONSI	ACE/ MILITARY	INDIVIDUAL ASSESSMENT	ASSESSMENT OF CERTIFICATES
UNIVERSITY OF TENNESSEE-MARTIN	X	X	X			X		X		
UNIVERSITY OF TENNESSEE-MEMPHIS										

TX INSTITUTION	ANY PRIOR LEARNING ASSESSMENT	ADVANCED PLACEMENT	CLEP	ACT/PEP	DANTES	CHALLENGE EXAM	ACE/ PONSI	ACE/ MILITARY	INDIVIDUAL ASSESSMENT	ASSESSMENT OF CERTIFICATES
ABILENE CHRISTIAN UNIVERSITY	X	X	X			X	X	X	X	
ALVIN COMMUNITY COLLEGE	X	X	X	X	X	X		X		X
AMBASSADOR UNIVERSITY	X	X	X					X		
ARLINGTON BAPTIST COLLEGE										
BAYLOR COLLEGE OF MEDICINE										
BAYLOR UNIVERSITY	X	X	X		X	X		X		
BLINN COLLEGE	X		X							
CEDAR VALLEY COLLEGE	X		X		X	X		X	X	
CENTRAL TEXAS COLLEGE	X	X	X	X	X	X	X	X	X	X
COLLIN COUNTY COMMUNITY COLLEGE-CENTRAL PARK	X	X	X	X	X	X	X	X	X	
COMMONWEALTH INSTITUTE OF FUNERAL SERVICE	X		X							
DALLAS BAPTIST UNIVERSITY	X	X	X	X	X	X	X	X	X	
DALLAS THEOLOGICAL SEMINARY	X					X				
EASTFIELD COLLEGE	X	X	X		X	X	X	X	X	
EL CENTRO COLLEGE	X	X	X		X	X		X	X	
EPISCOPAL THEOLOGICAL SEMINARY OF THE SOUTHWEST										

TX

INSTITUTION	ANY PRIOR LEARNING ASSESSMENT	ADVANCED PLACEMENT	CLEP	ACT/PEP	DANTES	CHALLENGE EXAM	ACE/ PONSI	ACE/ MILITARY	INDIVIDUAL ASSESSMENT	ASSESSMENT OF CERTIFICATES
HARDIN-SIMMONS UNIVERSITY	X	X	X		X	X		X		
HOUSTON COMMUNITY COLLEGE SYSTEM	X	X	X		X	X		X	X	X
HOWARD COUNTY JUNIOR COLLEGE DISTRICT	X	X	X			X		X		
HOWARD PAYNE UNIVERSITY	X	X	X	X	X	X	X	X	X	
JARVIS CHRISTIAN COLLEGE	X	X	X							
LAMAR UNIVERSITY-BEAUMONT	X		X		X	X	X	X	X	
LAREDO COMMUNITY COLLEGE	X	X	X			X				
LETOURNEAU UNIVERSITY	X	X	X	X	X		X	X	X	X
MCMURRY UNIVERSITY	X	X	X	X	X	X		X		
MIDLAND COLLEGE	X	X	X			X		X	X	X
MIDWESTERN STATE UNIVERSITY	X	X	X		X	X		X	X	
MOUNTAIN VIEW COLLEGE	X		X		X	X		X	X	X
NORTH CENTRAL TEXAS COLLEGE	X	X	X	X	X	X		X	X	
NORTH HARRIS MONTGOMERY COMMUNITY COLLEGE DISTRICT	X	X	X	X		X	X	X	X	X
OBLATE SCHOOL OF THEOLOGY	X					X	X			
OUR LADY OF THE LAKE UNIVERSITY- SAN ANTONIO	X	X	X	X	X	X		X	X	
SAINT EDWARDS UNIVERSITY	X	X	X	X	X	X	X		X	
SAM HOUSTON STATE UNIVERSITY	X	X	X		X			X		
SCHREINER COLLEGE										

TX

INSTITUTION	ANY PRIOR LEARNING ASSESSMENT	ADVANCED PLACEMENT	CLEP	ACT/PEP	DANTES	CHALLENGE EXAM	ACE/PONSI	ACE/MILITARY	INDIVIDUAL ASSESSMENT	ASSESSMENT OF CERTIFICATES
SOUTH TEXAS COLLEGE OF LAW										
SOUTHWESTERN UNIVERSITY	X	X				X		X		
STEPHEN F. AUSTIN STATE UNIVERSITY	X	X	X			X		X	X	
TEXAS A & M UNIVERSITY	X	X	X	X	X	X		X		
TEXAS CHRISTIAN UNIVERSITY	X	X	X						X	
TEXAS LUTHERAN COLLEGE	X	X	X	X	X	X		X		
TEXAS TECH UNIVERSITY	X	X	X	X		X				
TEXAS WESLEYAN UNIVERSITY	X	X	X			X			X	
THE UNIVERSITY OF TEXAS AT AUSTIN	X	X	X					X		
THE UNIVERSITY OF TEXAS AT DALLAS	X	X	X		X					
THE UNIVERSITY OF TEXAS AT EL PASO	X	X	X		X	X		X		X
THE UNIVERSITY OF TEXAS MEDICAL BRANCH-GALVESTON										
TRINITY UNIVERSITY	X	X				X		X		
TRINITY VALLEY COMMUNITY COLLEGE	X	X	X	X				X		
TYLER JUNIOR COLLEGE	X	X	X		X	X		X	X	
UNIVERSITY OF HOUSTON-UNIVERSITY PARK	X	X	X		X	X				
VERNON REGIONAL JUNIOR COLLEGE	X	X	X	X	X	X	X	X		
VICTORIA COLLEGE	X	X	X	X	X	X				
WAYLAND BAPTIST UNIVERSITY	X	X	X	X	X	X	X	X	X	X

	INSTITUTION	ANY PRIOR LEARNING ASSESSMENT	ADVANCED PLACEMENT	CLEP	ACT/PEP	DANTES	CHALLENGE EXAM	ACE/ PONSI	ACE/ MILITARY	INDIVIDUAL ASSESSMENT	ASSESSMENT OF CERTIFICATES
TX	WEST TEXAS A & M UNIVERSITY	X	X	X			X		X		
	WESTERN TEXAS COLLEGE	X	X	X	X				X		
UT	COLLEGE OF EASTERN UTAH	X		X		X	X		X		
	SNOW COLLEGE	X	X	X		X	X	X	X		
	SOUTHERN UTAH UNIVERSITY	X	X	X			X		X		
	UTAH STATE UNIVERSITY	X	X	X			X		X		
	UTAH VALLEY STATE COLLEGE	X	X	X	X	X	X		X	X	X
	WEBER STATE UNIVERSITY	X	X	X			X		X		
VA	BLUEFIELD COLLEGE	X	X	X		X		X	X	X	X
	BRIDGEWATER COLLEGE	X	X							X	
	CENTRAL VIRGINIA COMMUNITY COLLEGE	X	X	X		X	X	X	X	X	X
	CHRISTOPHER NEWPORT UNIVERSITY	X	X	X		X	X	X	X		
	COMMONWEALTH COLLEGE-VIRGINIA BEACH	X	X	X		X	X		X		
	EASTERN MENNONITE UNIVERSITY	X	X	X		X	X		X		
	EMORY AND HENRY COLLEGE										
	GERMANNA COMMUNITY COLLEGE	X	X	X			X	X	X		

VA

INSTITUTION	ANY PRIOR LEARNING ASSESSMENT	ADVANCED PLACEMENT	CLEP	ACT/PEP	DANTES	CHALLENGE EXAM	ACE/ PONSI	ACE/ MILITARY	INDIVIDUAL ASSESSMENT	ASSESSMENT OF CERTIFICATES
HAMPDEN-SYDNEY COLLEGE	X	X								
HAMPTON UNIVERSITY	X	X	X		X	X		X	X	
HOLLINS COLLEGE	X	X								
J. SARGEANT REYNOLDS COMMUNITY COLLEGE	X	X	X		X	X	X	X		
JAMES MADISON UNIVERSITY	X		X			X	X	X		
REGENT UNIVERSITY										
SHENANDOAH UNIVERSITY	X	X	X			X		X		
SWEET BRIAR COLLEGE	X	X								
THE UNIVERSITY OF CHARLESTON	X	X	X		X	X	X	X	X	X
THOMAS NELSON COMMUNITY COLLEGE	X	X	X		X	X		X	X	
UNION THEOLOGICAL SEMINARY IN VIRGINIA	X					X	X		X	
UNIVERSITY OF RICHMOND	X	X	X			X		X	X	
UNIVERSITY OF VIRGINIA-CLINCH VALLEY COLLEGE	X	X				X		X		
VIRGINIA MILITARY INSTITUTE	X	X						X		

VT

INSTITUTION	ANY PRIOR LEARNING ASSESSMENT	ADVANCED PLACEMENT	CLEP	ACT/PEP	DANTES	CHALLENGE EXAM	ACE/ PONSI	ACE/ MILITARY	INDIVIDUAL ASSESSMENT	ASSESSMENT OF CERTIFICATES
COLLEGE OF SAINT JOSEPH	X	X	X					X	X	X
GREEN MOUNTAIN COLLEGE	X	X	X	X	X	X	X	X	X	
LYNDON STATE COLLEGE	X	X	X	X	X		X	X	X	

VT

INSTITUTION	ANY PRIOR LEARNING ASSESSMENT	ADVANCED PLACEMENT	CLEP	ACT/PEP	DANTES	CHALLENGE EXAM	ACE/ PONSI	ACE/ MILITARY	INDIVIDUAL ASSESSMENT	ASSESSMENT OF CERTIFICATES
MARLBORO COLLEGE	X	X	X		X					
SAINT MICHAEL'S COLLEGE	X	X	X	X	X		X	X	X	
SCHOOL FOR INTERNATIONAL TRAINING	X	X	X	X	X		X	X		
TRINITY COLLEGE OF VERMONT	X	X	X	X	X		X	X	X	
VERMONT TECHNICAL COLLEGE	X	X	X		X	X		X	X	

WA

INSTITUTION	ANY PRIOR LEARNING ASSESSMENT	ADVANCED PLACEMENT	CLEP	ACT/PEP	DANTES	CHALLENGE EXAM	ACE/ PONSI	ACE/ MILITARY	INDIVIDUAL ASSESSMENT	ASSESSMENT OF CERTIFICATES
BIG BEND COMMUNITY COLLEGE	X	X	X	X	X	X		X	X	
CENTRAL WASHINGTON UNIVERSITY	X		X		X	X	X	X		
CORNISH COLLEGE OF THE ARTS										
EVERETT COMMUNITY COLLEGE	X	X	X		X	X		X	X	
GONZAGA UNIVERSITY	X	X	X	X		X		X		
GREEN RIVER COMMUNITY COLLEGE	X	X	X		X	X	X	X	X	
HENRY COGSWELL COLLEGE	X		X	X		X	X	X	X	
HIGHLINE COMMUNITY COLLEGE	X	X				X		X		
LUTHERAN BIBLE INSTITUTE OF SEATTLE	X	X	X	X	X		X	X	X	
NORTHWEST COLLEGE OF THE ASSEMBLIES OF GOD	X	X	X		X	X	X	X	X	
PACIFIC LUTHERAN UNIVERSITY	X	X	X	X	X	X	X	X	X	
PUGET SOUND CHRISTIAN COLLEGE	X	X	X	X	X	X	X	X	X	
RENTON TECHNICAL COLLEGE	X		X						X	

INSTITUTION	ANY PRIOR LEARNING ASSESSMENT	ADVANCED PLACEMENT	CLEP	ACT/PEP	DANTES	CHALLENGE EXAM	ACE/ PONSI	ACE/ MILITARY	INDIVIDUAL ASSESSMENT	ASSESSMENT OF CERTIFICATES
SPOKANE FALLS COMMUNITY COLLEGE	X	X			X	X		X		
TACOMA COMMUNITY COLLEGE	X	X	X			X		X		
UNIVERSITY OF PUGET SOUND										
WALLA WALLA COLLEGE	X	X	X			X				
WASHINGTON STATE UNIVERSITY	X	X	X		X	X	X	X		
WENATCHEE VALLEY COLLEGE	X		X			X		X		
WESTERN WASHINGTON UNIVERSITY	X	X				X		X		
WHATCOM COMMUNITY COLLEGE	X	X	X	X	X	X	X	X	X	
WHITMAN COLLEGE	X					X		X		

INSTITUTION	ANY PRIOR LEARNING ASSESSMENT	ADVANCED PLACEMENT	CLEP	ACT/PEP	DANTES	CHALLENGE EXAM	ACE/ PONSI	ACE/ MILITARY	INDIVIDUAL ASSESSMENT	ASSESSMENT OF CERTIFICATES
ALVERNO COLLEGE	X	X	X			X			X	
BELLIN COLLEGE OF NURSING	X	X	X	X		X			X	X
BELOIT COLLEGE	X	X	X	X	X	X		X	X	
CARDINAL STRITCH COLLEGE	X		X	X	X	X	X	X	X	X
CARROLL COLLEGE	X	X	X	X		X				
CARTHAGE COLLEGE	X	X	X	X		X		X		
CHIPPEWA VALLEY TECHNICAL COLLEGE	X		X		X	X		X	X	
CONCORDIA UNIVERSITY-WISCONSIN	X	X	X	X	X	X	X	X	X	
EDGEWOOD COLLEGE	X		X	X	X	X	X	X	X	

WI INSTITUTION	ANY PRIOR LEARNING ASSESSMENT	ADVANCED PLACEMENT	CLEP	ACT/PEP	DANTES	CHALLENGE EXAM	ACE/PONSI	ACE/MILITARY	INDIVIDUAL ASSESSMENT	ASSESSMENT OF CERTIFICATES
FOX VALLEY TECHNICAL COLLEGE	X		X	X		X			X	
LAWRENCE UNIVERSITY	X	X				X				
MARANATHA BAPTIST BIBLE COLLEGE INC	X		X		X			X		
MARIAN COLLEGE OF FOND DU LAC	X	X	X	X	X	X	X	X	X	
MID-STATE TECHNICAL COLLEGE-MAIN CAMPUS										
MOUNT MARY COLLEGE	X	X	X		X	X	X		X	
MOUNT SENARIO COLLEGE	X	X	X	X	X	X	X	X	X	
NASHOTAH HOUSE										
NORTHLAND COLLEGE	X	X	X		X	X	X	X	X	
RIPON COLLEGE	X	X						X		
SACRED HEART SCHOOL OF THEOLOGY	X								X	
SAINT NORBERT COLLEGE	X	X	X	X	X		X	X	X	
SILVER LAKE COLLEGE	X	X	X				X	X	X	
UNIVERSITY OF WISCONSIN-EAU CLAIRE	X	X	X	X	X	X		X	X	
UNIVERSITY OF WISCONSIN-LA CROSSE	X	X	X		X	X		X		
UNIVERSITY OF WISCONSIN-MADISON	X		X		X	X				
UNIVERSITY OF WISCONSIN-PARKSIDE	X	X	X		X	X		X		
UNIVERSITY OF WISCONSIN-PLATTEVILLE	X	X	X		X	X		X		
UNIVERSITY OF WISCONSIN-RIVER FALLS	X	X	X	X	X	X	X	X	X	

WI

INSTITUTION	ANY PRIOR LEARNING ASSESSMENT	ADVANCED PLACEMENT	CLEP	ACT/PEP	DANTES	CHALLENGE EXAM	ACE/ PONSI	ACE/ MILITARY	INDIVIDUAL ASSESSMENT	ASSESSMENT OF CERTIFICATES
UNIVERSITY OF WISCONSIN-STEVENS POINT	X	X	X		X	X	X	X	X	
UNIVERSITY OF WISCONSIN-STOUT	X	X	X	X	X	X	X	X	X	X
UNIVERSITY OF WISCONSIN-SUPERIOR	X	X	X		X	X	X	X	X	
UNIVERSITY OF WISCONSIN-WHITEWATER	X	X	X		X	X				
VITERBO COLLEGE	X	X	X		X	X		X	X	
WAUKESHA COUNTY TECHNICAL COLLEGE	X		X			X		X	X	X
WISCONSIN LUTHERAN COLLEGE	X	X	X		X	X			X	
WISCONSIN SCHOOL OF PROFESSIONAL PSYCHOLOGY										

WV

INSTITUTION	ANY PRIOR LEARNING ASSESSMENT	ADVANCED PLACEMENT	CLEP	ACT/PEP	DANTES	CHALLENGE EXAM	ACE/ PONSI	ACE/ MILITARY	INDIVIDUAL ASSESSMENT	ASSESSMENT OF CERTIFICATES
BLUEFIELD STATE COLLEGE	X	X	X		X	X		X	X	X
DAVIS AND ELKINS COLLEGE	X	X	X	X	X	X	X	X	X	X
FAIRMONT STATE COLLEGE	X	X	X		X	X	X	X	X	X
SHEPHERD COLLEGE	X	X	X		X	X		X	X	X
THE COLLEGE OF WEST VIRGINIA	X	X	X	X	X	X	X	X	X	X
WEST VIRGINIA STATE COLLEGE	X	X	X	X	X	X	X	X	X	X
WEST VIRGINIA UNIVERSITY AT PARKERSBURG	X	X	X			X		X		X

INSTITUTION	ANY PRIOR LEARNING ASSESSMENT	ADVANCED PLACEMENT	CLEP	ACT/PEP	DANTES	CHALLENGE EXAM	ACE/ PONSI	ACE/ MILITARY	INDIVIDUAL ASSESSMENT	ASSESSMENT OF CERTIFICATES
BOARD OF TRUSTEES-STATE INSTS OF HIGHER LEARNING										
COLUMBIA COLLEGE	X					X		X	X	
INTER AMERICAN UNIV OF PUERTO RICO-CENTRAL OFFICE	X	X	X		X	X		X	X	
PONCE SCHOOL OF MEDICINE										
UNIVERSIDADMETROPOLITANA	X		X			X		X		
UNIVERSITY OF PUERTO RICO-CAYEY UNIVERSITY COLLEGE	X	X								
UNIVERSITY OF PUERTO RICO-CENTRAL ADMINISTRATION	X		X	X						
UNIVERSITY OF PUERTO RICO-HUMACAO UNIVERSITY COLLEGE	X	X				X				
UNIVERSITY OF PUERTO RICO-RIO PIEDRAS CAMPUS	X	X								
UNIVERSITY OF SACRED HEART	X	X				X		X	X	

1996 Prior Learning Assessment Survey
[By Carnegie Classification]

INSTITUTION	ANY PRIOR LEARNING ASSESSMENT	ADVANCED PLACEMENT	CLEP	ACT/PEP	DANTES	CHALLENGE EXAM	ACE/PONSI	ACE/MILITARY	INDIVIDUAL ASSESSMENT	ASSESSMENT OF CERTIFICATES
RESEARCH UNIVERSITIES I										
CALIFORNIA INSTITUTE OF TECHNOLOGY—CA										
CARNEGIE MELLON UNIVERSITY—PA										
FLORIDA STATE UNIVERSITY—FL	X	X	X		X	X		X		
GEORGIA INSTITUTE OF TECHNOLOGY-MAIN CAMPUS—GA										
INDIANA UNIVERSITY-BLOOMINGTON—IN	X	X	X		X	X	X	X	X	X
IOWA STATE UNIVERSITY—IA	X	X	X		X	X	X	X		
JOHNS HOPKINS UNIVERSITY—MD	X									
LOUISIANA ST UNIV & AGRL & MECH & HEBERT LAWS CT—LA	X	X	X			X	X	X		
MICHIGAN STATE UNIVERSITY—MI	X	X	X			X				
NORTHWESTERN UNIVERSITY—IL	X	X	X							
OHIO STATE UNIVERSITY-MAIN CAMPUS—OH	X	X	X		X	X	X	X	X	
OREGON STATE UNIVERSITY—OR										
PRINCETON UNIVERSITY—NJ										
RUTGERS UNIVERSITY-NEW BRUNSWICK—NJ	X	X	X	X	X	X				
STANFORD UNIVERSITY—CA	X	X								

INSTITUTION	ANY PRIOR LEARNING ASSESSMENT	ADVANCED PLACEMENT	CLEP	ACT/PEP	DANTES	CHALLENGE EXAM	ACE/ PONSI	ACE/MILITARY	INDIVIDUAL ASSESSMENT	ASSESSMENT OF CERTIFICATES
TEMPLE UNIVERSITY—PA	X	X	X							
TEXAS A & M UNIVERSITY—TX	X	X	X	X	X	X		X		
THE UNIVERSITY OF TEXAS AT AUSTIN—TX	X	X	X					X		
UNIVERSITY OF CALIFORNIA-DAVIS—CA	X	X				X				
UNIVERSITY OF CALIFORNIA-LOS ANGELES—CA	X	X						X		
UNIVERSITY OF CALIFORNIA-SANTA BARBARA—CA	X	X								
UNIVERSITY OF CINCINNATI-MAIN CAMPUS—OH	X	X	X	X		X			X	
UNIVERSITY OF FLORIDA—FL	X	X	X			X				
UNIVERSITY OF GEORGIA—GA	X	X	X		X	X	X	X	X	
UNIVERSITY OF IOWA—IA	X	X	X	X		X	X	X		
UNIVERSITY OF KANSAS-MAIN CAMPUS—KS	X	X	X		X	X		X		
UNIVERSITY OF KENTUCKY—KY	X	X	X		X	X	X	X		
UNIVERSITY OF MARYLAND-COLLEGE PARK CAMPUS—MD	X	X	X			X				
UNIVERSITY OF MASSACHUSETTS-AMHERST—MA	X	X	X	X	X	X	X	X	X	
UNIVERSITY OF MIAMI—FL	X	X	X		X	X				
UNIVERSITY OF MINNESOTA-TWIN CITIES—MN	X	X	X	X	X	X		X	X	
UNIVERSITY OF NEBRASKA AT LINCOLN—NE	X	X	X		X	X		X	X	
UNIVERSITY OF SOUTHERN CALIFORNIA—CA	X			X				X		

INSTITUTION	ANY PRIOR LEARNING ASSESSMENT	ADVANCED PLACEMENT	CLEP	ACT/PEP	DANTES	CHALLENGE EXAM	ACE/PONSI	ACE/MILITARY	INDIVIDUAL ASSESSMENT	ASSESSMENT OF CERTIFICATES
UNIVERSITY OF TENNESSEE-KNOXVILLE—TN	X	X	X		X	X		X		
UNIVERSITY OF WISCONSIN-MADISON—WI	X		X		X	X				
UTAH STATE UNIVERSITY—UT	X	X	X			X		X		
WAYNE STATE UNIVERSITY—MI	X	X	X		X	X				
YALE UNIVERSITY—CT										
RESEARCH UNIVERSITIES II										
AUBURN UNIVERSITY-MAIN CAMPUS—AL	X	X	X			X				
CLEMSON UNIVERSITY—SC	X					X				
KANSAS STATE UNIVERSITY OF AGRICULTURE AND APPS—KS	X	X	X	X	X	X		X	X	
KENT STATE UNIVERSITY-MAIN CAMPUS—OH	X	X	X		X	X	X	X	X	
MISSISSIPPI STATE UNIVERSITY—MS	X	X	X			X		X		
NORTHEASTERN UNIVERSITY—MA	X	X	X	X	X	X	X	X	X	X
OHIO UNIVERSITY-MAIN CAMPUS—OH	X	X	X			X		X	X	
OKLAHOMA STATE UNIVERSITY- MAIN CAMPUS—OK	X	X	X	X	X	X	X	X		
RENSSELAER POLYTECHNIC INSTITUTE—NY	X	X						X		
SAINT LOUIS UNIVERSITY-MAIN CAMPUS—MO	X	X	X	X	X	X		X	X	
SYRACUSE UNIVERSITY—NY	X	X	X		X	X	X	X	X	
TEXAS TECH UNIVERSITY—TX	X	X	X	X		X				

INSTITUTION	ANY PRIOR LEARNING ASSESSMENT	ADVANCED PLACEMENT	CLEP	ACT/PEP	DANTES	CHALLENGE EXAM	ACE/PONSI	ACE/MILITARY	INDIVIDUAL ASSESSMENT	ASSESSMENT OF CERTIFICATES
UNIVERSITY OF HOUSTON-UNIVERSITY PARK—TX	X		X		X	X				
UNIVERSITY OF OREGON—OR										
WASHINGTON STATE UNIVERSITY—WA	X	X	X		X	X	X	X		
DOCTORAL UNIVERSITIES I										
BOSTON COLLEGE—MA	X	X								
BOWLING GREEN STATE UNIVERSITY-MAIN CAMPUS—OH	X	X			X	X		X	X	
CATHOLIC UNIVERSITY OF AMERICA—DC	X	X	X							
CLARK ATLANTA UNIVERSITY—GA	X	X	X							
DREXEL UNIVERSITY—PA	X		X			X			X	
FLORIDA INSTITUTE OF TECHNOLOGY—FL	X	X	X			X				
FORDHAM UNIVERSITY—NY	X	X	X						X	
GEORGIA STATE UNIVERSITY—GA	X	X	X		X	X				
ILLINOIS STATE UNIVERSITY—IL	X		X		X			X	X	
NORTHERN ARIZONA UNIVERSITY—AZ	X	X	X	X	X	X			X	
THE UNION INSTITUTE—OH	X	X	X	X	X	X		X	X	
THE UNIVERSITY OF TEXAS AT DALLAS—TX	X	X	X		X					
UNIVERSITY OF AKRON-MAIN CAMPUS—OH	X	X	X		X	X		X		
UNIVERSITY OF DENVER—CO	X	X	X					X		

INSTITUTION	ANY PRIOR LEARNING ASSESSMENT	ADVANCED PLACEMENT	CLEP	ACT/PEP	DANTES	CHALLENGE EXAM	ACE/PONSI	ACE/MILITARY	INDIVIDUAL ASSESSMENT	ASSESSMENT OF CERTIFICATES
UNIVERSITY OF MISSOURI-KANSAS CITY—MI	X	X	X	X		X		X		
UNIVERSITY OF NORTHERN COLORADO—CO	X	X	X		X	X		X		
DOCTORAL UNIVERSITIES II										
BAYLOR UNIVERSITY—TX	X	X	X		X	X		X		
BIOLA UNIVERSITY—CA	X	X	X		X	X	X	X	X	X
CLEVELAND STATE UNIVERSITY—OH	X	X	X		X	X	X	X	X	
COLORADO SCHOOL OF MINES—CO	X	X				X		X		
DARTMOUTH COLLEGE—NH	X	X								
FLORIDA ATLANTIC UNIVERSITY—FL	X	X	X	X	X					
FLORIDA INTERNATIONAL UNIVERSITY—FL	X	X	X		X			X		
INDIANA UNIVERSITY-PURDUE UNIVERSITY-INDIANAPOLIS—IN	X	X	X		X	X	X	X	X	X
MONTANA STATE UNIVERSITY-BOZEMAN—MT	X	X	X			X		X		
NORTH DAKOTA STATE UNIVERSITY-MAIN CAMPUS—ND	X	X	X		X	X	X	X	X	
PACE UNIVERSITY-NEW YORK—NY	X	X	X	X	X	X	X	X	X	X
PEPPERDINE UNIVERSITY—CA	X	X	X			X	X	X		
PORTLAND STATE UNIVERSITY—OR	X	X	X		X	X		X		
SUNY COLLEGE OF ENVIRONMENTAL SCIENCE AND FOREST—NY	X	X	X	X	X		X	X	X	
TEXAS CHRISTIAN UNIVERSITY—TX	X	X	X						X	

INSTITUTION	ANY PRIOR LEARNING ASSESSMENT	ADVANCED PLACEMENT	CLEP	ACT/PEP	DANTES	CHALLENGE EXAM	ACE/ PONSI	ACE/MILITARY	INDIVIDUAL ASSESSMENT	ASSESSMENT OF CERTIFICATES
THE UNIVERSITY OF MONTANA-MISSOULA—MT	X	X	X		X	X	X	X		
UNIVERSITY OF CENTRAL FLORIDA—FL										X
UNIVERSITY OF LAVERNE—CA	X	X	X	X	X	X	X	X	X	
UNIVERSITY OF MAINE—ME	X	X	X			X			X	
UNIVERSITY OF NEW HAMPSHIRE-MAIN CAMPUS—NH	X	X	X	X		X		X		
UNIVERSITY OF NEW ORLEANS—LA	X	X	X			X	X	X		
UNIVERSITY OF NORTH DAKOTA-MAIN CAMPUS—ND	X	X	X	X	X	X		X	X	
UNIVERSITY OF PUERTO RICO-RIO PIEDRAS CAMPUS—PR	X	X								
UNIVERSITY OF SAN FRANCISCO—CA	X	X	X		X	X	X	X	X	
UNIVERSITY OF SOUTH DAKOTA—SD	X	X	X		X	X		X		
UNIVERSITY OF TULSA—OK	X	X	X	X		X				
WICHITA STATE UNIVERSITY—KS	X	X	X		X	X		X	X	
WRIGHT STATE UNIVERSITY-MAIN CAMPUS—OH	X	X	X	X	X	X	X	X		
MASTER'S (COMPREHENSIVE) UNIVERSITIES AND COLLEGES										
ABILENE CHRISTIAN UNIVERSITY—TX	X	X	X			X	X	X	X	
ALBANY STATE COLLEGE—GA	X	X	X		X	X		X		
AMERICAN INTERNATIONAL COLLEGE—MA										

INSTITUTION	ANY PRIOR LEARNING ASSESSMENT	ADVANCED PLACEMENT	CLEP	ACT/PEP	DANTES	CHALLENGE EXAM	ACE/ PONSI	ACE/MILITARY	INDIVIDUAL ASSESSMENT	ASSESSMENT OF CERTIFICATES
ARKANSAS STATE UNIVERSITY- MAIN CAMPUS—AR	X	X	X	X	X	X	X	X		
ARKANSAS TECH UNIVERSITY—AR	X	X	X	X		X		X		
ARMSTRONG STATE COLLEGE—GA	X	X	X	X	X			X		
ASHLAND UNIVERSITY—OH	X	X	X	X	X	X	X	X		
ASSUMPTION COLLEGE—MA	X	X	X	X	X		X	X	X	
AUBURN UNIVERSITY AT MONTGOMERY—AL	X	X	X	X	X	X	X	X		
AURORA UNIVERSITY—IL	X		X	X	X	X		X	X	
AUSTIN PEAY STATE UNIVERSITY—TN	X	X	X	X	X	X	X	X		
AZUSA PACIFIC UNIVERSITY—CA	X	X	X	X	X	X	X	X	X	
BALDWIN-WALLACE COLLEGE—OH	X	X	X		X		X	X	X	
BARRY UNIVERSITY—FL	X	X	X		X	X	X	X	X	X
BEAVER COLLEGE—PA	X	X	X	X		X	X	X		
BELLARMINE COLLEGE—KY	X	X	X	X	X	X	X	X	X	
BLOOMSBURG UNIVERSITY OF PENNSYLVANIA—PA	X	X	X			X		X	X	
BOISE STATE UNIVERSITY—ID	X	X	X	X	X	X	X	X	X	
BRENAU UNIVERSITY—GA	X	X	X	X	X	X		X	X	
BRIDGEWATER STATE COLLEGE—MA	X	X	X	X	X	X		X		
BUTLER UNIVERSITY—IN	X	X	X	X	X			X		

INSTITUTION	ANY PRIOR LEARNING ASSESSMENT	ADVANCED PLACEMENT	CLEP	ACT/PEP	DANTES	CHALLENGE EXAM	ACE/ PONSI	ACE/MILITARY	INDIVIDUAL ASSESSMENT	ASSESSMENT OF CERTIFICATES
CALIFORNIA LUTHERAN UNIVERSITY—CA	X		X			X		X	X	
CALIFORNIA STATE UNIVERSITY-BAKERSFIELD—CA	X	X	X		X	X		X	X	
CAMPBELL UNIVERSITY INC—NC	X	X	X	X	X	X	X	X	X	
CANISIUS COLLEGE—NY	X	X	X	X	X	X			X	
CARDINAL STRITCH COLLEGE—WI	X	X	X	X	X	X	X	X	X	X
CENTRAL MICHIGAN UNIVERSITY—MI	X	X	X	X			X	X	X	X
CENTRAL MISSOURI STATE UNIVERSITY—MO	X	X	X			X		X	X	X
CENTRAL WASHINGTON UNIVERSITY—WA	X		X		X	X	X	X		
CHAMINADE UNIVERSITY OF HONOLULU—HI	X	X	X		X	X		X	X	
CHAPMAN UNIVERSITY—CA	X	X	X		X	X	X	X		X
COLLEGE OF NEW ROCHELLE—NY	X		X						X	
COLLEGE OF NOTRE DAME—CA	X	X	X	X	X	X	X	X		
COLLEGE OF SAINT FRANCIS—IL	X	X	X			X	X	X	X	
COLLEGE OF SAINT ROSE—NY	X	X	X						X	
CONCORDIA UNIVERSITY—IL	X	X	X	X	X	X	X	X	X	X
CONVERSE COLLEGE—SC	X	X				X			X	
CREIGHTON UNIVERSITY—NE	X	X	X	X	X	X		X	X	
CUNY BROOKLYN COLLEGE—NY	X	X	X	X	X	X		X	X	

INSTITUTION	ANY PRIOR LEARNING ASSESSMENT	ADVANCED PLACEMENT	CLEP	ACT/PEP	DANTES	CHALLENGE EXAM	ACE/PONSI	ACE/MILITARY	INDIVIDUAL ASSESSMENT	ASSESSMENT OF CERTIFICATES
CUNY COLLEGE OF STATEN ISLAND—NY	X	X	X		X	X			X	
CUNY LEHMAN COLLEGE—NY	X	X	X	X	X	X	X	X	X	
DALLAS BAPTIST UNIVERSITY—TX	X	X	X	X	X	X	X	X	X	
EAST STROUDSBURG UNIVERSITY OF PENNSYLVANIA—PA	X	X	X			X				
EAST TENNESSEE STATE UNIVERSITY—TN	X	X	X	X	X	X	X	X	X	
EASTERN MICHIGAN UNIVERSITY—MI	X	X	X					X	X	X
EDGEWOOD COLLEGE—WI	X		X	X	X	X	X	X	X	
EDINBORO UNIVERSITY OF PENNSYLVANIA—PA	X	X	X	X		X		X	X	X
EMBRY-RIDDLE AERONAUTICAL UNIVERSITY—FL	X	X	X	X	X	X		X	X	
EMERSON COLLEGE—MA	X	X	X							
EMMANUEL COLLEGE—MA	X	X	X	X	X	X	X	X	X	
EMPORIA STATE UNIVERSITY—KS	X	X	X	X	X	X		X		
FITCHBURG STATE COLLEGE—MA	X	X	X	X	X	X	X	X		
FONTBONNE COLLEGE—MO	X	X	X			X	X	X	X	X
FORT HAYS STATE UNIVERSITY—KS	X	X	X	X		X		X		
FRANCISCAN UNIVERSITY OF STEUBENVILLE—OH	X	X	X	X		X		X		
GALLAUDET UNIVERSITY—DC	X	X	X							
GARDNER-WEBB UNIVERSITY—NC	X	X	X	X	X	X		X		

INSTITUTION	ANY PRIOR LEARNING ASSESSMENT	ADVANCED PLACEMENT	CLEP	ACT/PEP	DANTES	CHALLENGE EXAM	ACE/ PONSI	ACE/MILITARY	INDIVIDUAL ASSESSMENT	ASSESSMENT OF CERTIFICATES
GEORGIAN COURT COLLEGE—NJ	X	X	X		X		X	X		
GONZAGA UNIVERSITY—WA	X	X	X	X		X		X		
GOVERNORS STATE UNIVERSITY—IL	X		X	X	X		X	X	X	
GRAND VALLEY STATE UNIVERSITY—MI	X	X	X					X		
HAMPTON UNIVERSITY—VA	X	X	X		X	X		X	X	
HARDIN-SIMMONS UNIVERSITY—TX	X	X	X		X	X		X		
HAWAII PACIFIC UNIVERSITY—HI	X	X	X	X	X	X	X	X		X
HOLY NAMES COLLEGE—CA	X	X	X		X	X		X	X	
HOOD COLLEGE—MD	X	X	X			X	X	X	X	
HUMBOLDT STATE UNIVERSITY—CA	X	X	X			X		X	X	
ILLINOIS BENEDICTINE COLLEGE—IL	X	X	X	X					X	
IMMACULATA COLLEGE—PA	X	X	X	X	X	X	X	X	X	X
INDIANA UNIVERSITY-SOUTH BEND—IN	X	X	X		X	X	X	X	X	
IONA COLLEGE—NY	X	X	X			X	X	X	X	
ITHACA COLLEGE—NY	X	X	X	X	X			X		
JAMES MADISON UNIVERSITY—VA	X		X			X	X	X		
LA ROCHE COLLEGE—PA	X	X	X	X	X	X	X	X	X	X
LA SALLE UNIVERSITY—PA	X	X	X	X	X	X	X	X		
LA SIERRA UNIVERSITY—CA	X	X	X	X	X	X		X	X	

INSTITUTION	ANY PRIOR LEARNING ASSESSMENT	ADVANCED PLACEMENT	CLEP	ACT/PEP	DANTES	CHALLENGE EXAM	ACE/PONSI	ACE/MILITARY	INDIVIDUAL ASSESSMENT	ASSESSMENT OF CERTIFICATES
LAMAR UNIVERSITY-BEAUMONT—TX	X		X		X	X	X	X	X	
LESLEY COLLEGE—MA	X	X	X	X	X		X	X	X	X
LEWIS UNIVERSITY—IL	X	X	X		X	X	X	X	X	
LINCOLN MEMORIAL UNIVERSITY—TN	X	X	X			X		X	X	
LOYOLA COLLEGE—MD	X	X	X			X	X			
MADONNA UNIVERSITY—MI	X	X	X			X	X	X	X	X
MAHARISHI UNIVERSITY OF MANAGEMENT—IA	X	X	X	X	X			X	X	
MANKATO STATE UNIVERSITY—MN	X		X	X	X	X		X		
MARIST COLLEGE—NY	X	X	X	X	X			X	X	
MARYWOOD COLLEGE—PA	X	X	X	X	X	X	X	X	X	
MCNEESE STATE UNIVERSITY—LA	X	X	X	X		X		X		
MIDWESTERN STATE UNIVERSITY—TX	X	X	X		X	X		X	X	
MISSISSIPPI COLLEGE—MS	X	X	X		X	X		X		
MONTANA STATE UNIVERSITY-BILLINGS—MT	X	X	X	X	X	X	X	X		
MONTANA STATE UNIVERSITY-NORTHERN—MT	X	X	X		X			X	X	
MONTCLAIR STATE UNIVERSITY—NJ	X	X	X			X		X	X	
MOORHEAD STATE UNIVERSITY—MN	X		X			X			X	X
MORGAN STATE UNIVERSITY—MD	X	X	X					X		
MURRAY STATE UNIVERSITY—KY	X	X	X		X	X	X	X	X	

INSTITUTION	ANY PRIOR LEARNING ASSESSMENT	ADVANCED PLACEMENT	CLEP	ACT/PEP	DANTES	CHALLENGE EXAM	ACE/ PONSI	ACE/MILITARY	INDIVIDUAL ASSESSMENT	ASSESSMENT OF CERTIFICATES
NATIONAL UNIVERSITY—CA	X		X	X	X	X	X	X		X
NATIONAL-LOUIS UNIVERSITY—IL	X		X	X	X	X	X	X	X	X
NEW YORK INSTITUTE OF TECHNOLOGY-OLD WESTBURY—NY	X	X	X	X	X	X	X	X	X	X
NIAGARA UNIVERSITY—NY	X	X	X			X		X	X	X
NORTH CAROLINA CENTRAL UNIVERSITY—NC	X		X			X		X		
NORTH GEORGIA COLLEGE—GA	X	X	X		X	X		X		
NORTHERN KENTUCKY UNIVERSITY—KY	X	X	X			X	X	X	X	
NORTHERN STATE UNIVERSITY—SD	X	X	X		X	X	X	X		
NOTRE DAME COLLEGE—NH	X	X	X		X	X	X	X	X	
OLIVET NAZARENE UNIVERSITY—IL	X	X	X	X	X	X	X	X	X	
OUR LADY OF THE LAKE UNIVERSITY-SAN ANTONIO—TX	X	X	X	X	X	X		X	X	
PACIFIC LUTHERAN UNIVERSITY—WA	X	X	X	X	X	X	X	X	X	
PEMBROKE STATE UNIVERSITY—NC	X	X	X		X			X		
PITTSBURG STATE UNIVERSITY—KS	X	X	X		X	X		X		
PLYMOUTH STATE COLLEGE—NH	X	X	X		X	X		X		
PURDUE UNIVERSITY-CALUMET CAMPUS—IN	X	X	X			X			X	
REGIS UNIVERSITY—CO	X	X	X	X	X	X	X	X	X	X
RIVIER COLLEGE—NH	X	X	X	X	X	X	X	X	X	

INSTITUTION	ANY PRIOR LEARNING ASSESSMENT	ADVANCED PLACEMENT	CLEP	ACT/PEP	DANTES	CHALLENGE EXAM	ACE/ PONSI	ACE/MILITARY	INDIVIDUAL ASSESSMENT	ASSESSMENT OF CERTIFICATES
ROCHESTER INSTITUTE OF TECHNOLOGY—NY	X	X	X	X	X	X	X	X	X	
ROCKFORD COLLEGE—IL	X		X					X		
ROCKHURST COLLEGE—MO	X	X	X		X			X		
ROOSEVELT UNIVERSITY—IL	X	X	X		X	X		X		
ROSARY COLLEGE—IL	X	X	X		X			X	X	
SACRED HEART UNIVERSITY—CT	X	X	X	X	X		X	X	X	
SAGINAW VALLEY STATE UNIVERSITY—MI	X		X	X	X	X				
SAINT BONAVENTURE UNIVERSITY—NY	X	X	X							
SAINT FRANCIS COLLEGE—IN	X	X	X	X	X		X	X	X	
ST. FRANCIS COLLEGE—NY	X	X	X	X	X		X	X	X	
SAINT JOSEPH'S UNIVERSITY—PA	X	X				X				
SAINT MARY'S COLLEGE OF CALIFORNIA—CA	X	X	X	X	X	X	X	X	X	
SAINT MICHAEL'S COLLEGE—VT	X	X	X	X	X		X	X	X	
SAINT XAVIER UNIVERSITY—IL	X	X	X	X	X	X	X	X	X	
SALEM STATE COLLEGE—MA	X	X	X	X			X	X	X	
SAM HOUSTON STATE UNIVERSITY—TX	X	X	X		X			X		
SANTA CLARA UNIVERSITY—CA	X	X				X				
SHENANDOAH UNIVERSITY—VA	X	X	X			X		X		
SLIPPERY ROCK UNIVERSITY OF PENNSYLVANIA—PA	X	X	X	X	X	X		X		

INSTITUTION	ANY PRIOR LEARNING ASSESSMENT	ADVANCED PLACEMENT	CLEP	ACT/PEP	DANTES	CHALLENGE EXAM	ACE/PONSI	ACE/MILITARY	INDIVIDUAL ASSESSMENT	ASSESSMENT OF CERTIFICATES
SOUTH DAKOTA STATE UNIVERSITY—SD	X	X	X	X	X	X				
SOUTHEAST MISSOURI STATE UNIVERSITY—MO	X	X	X		X	X		X		
SOUTHERN NAZARENE UNIVERSITY—OK	X	X	X		X	X	X	X	X	X
SOUTHWESTERN OKLAHOMA STATE UNIVERSITY—OK	X	X	X		X	X	X	X		
SPALDING UNIVERSITY—KY	X	X	X	X		X	X	X	X	
STEPHEN F. AUSTIN STATE UNIVERSITY—TX	X	X	X			X		X	X	
STETSON UNIVERSITY—FL	X	X	X			X				
SUNY COLLEGE AT BROCKPORT—NY	X	X	X	X		X	X	X	X	
SUNY COLLEGE AT GENESEO—NY	X	X	X							
SUNY COLLEGE AT POTSDAM—NY	X	X	X		X		X	X		
TEXAS WESLEYAN UNIVERSITY—TX	X	X	X			X			X	
THE UNIVERSITY OF TEXAS AT EL PASO—TX	X	X	X		X	X		X		X
TOWSON STATE UNIVERSITY—MD	X	X	X	X		X		X	X	
TRENTON STATE COLLEGE—NJ	X	X	X		X	X		X		
TREVECCA NAZARENE COLLEGE—TN	X	X	X	X	X		X	X	X	X
TRINITY UNIVERSITY—TX	X	X				X		X		
TROY STATE UNIVERSITY AT DOTHAN—AL	X	X	X		X			X		
TUSKEGEE UNIVERSITY—AL	X	X	X					X		
UNIVERSITY OF ALASKA - ANCHORAGE—AK	X	X	X	X	X	X	X	X	X	

INSTITUTION	ANY PRIOR LEARNING ASSESSMENT	ADVANCED PLACEMENT	CLEP	ACT/PEP	DANTES	CHALLENGE EXAM	ACE/PONSI	ACE/MILITARY	INDIVIDUAL ASSESSMENT	ASSESSMENT OF CERTIFICATES
UNIVERSITY OF BRIDGEPORT—CT	X	X	X			X			X	
UNIVERSITY OF CENTRAL ARKANSAS—AR	X	X	X		X	X		X		
UNIVERSITY OF DAYTON—OH	X	X	X						X	
UNIVERSITY OF DUBUQUE—IA	X	X	X	X	X	X		X	X	
UNIVERSITY OF EVANSVILLE—IN	X		X		X	X	X	X	X	
UNIVERSITY OF ILLINIOS AT SPRINGFIELD—IL	X		X		X		X	X	X	
UNIVERSITY OF MARY—ND	X	X	X	X	X	X	X	X	X	X
UNIVERSITY OF MARYLAND UNIVERSITY COLLEGE—MD	X	X	X	X	X	X		X	X	
UNIVERSITY OF MINNESOTA-DULUTH—MN	X	X	X					X		
UNIVERSITY OF MONTEVALLO—AL	X	X	X			X		X		
UNIVERSITY OF NEBRASKA AT KEARNEY—NE	X		X			X	X	X	X	
UNIVERSITY OF NORTH ALABAMA—AL	X	X	X		X			X		
UNIVERSITY OF NORTH CAROLINA AT WILMINGTON—NC	X	X	X					X		
UNIVERSITY OF REDLANDS—CA	X		X		X	X		X	X	X
UNIVERSITY OF RICHMOND—VA	X	X	X			X		X	X	
UNIVERSITY OF SCRANTON—PA	X		X	X	X	X	X	X	X	X
UNIVERSITY OF SOUTH ALABAMA—AL	X	X	X		X	X	X	X		
UNIVERSITY OF SOUTHERN MAINE—ME	X	X	X		X	X	X	X	X	X

INSTITUTION	ANY PRIOR LEARNING ASSESSMENT	ADVANCED PLACEMENT	CLEP	ACT/PEP	DANTES	CHALLENGE EXAM	ACE/ PONSI	ACE/MILITARY	INDIVIDUAL ASSESSMENT	ASSESSMENT OF CERTIFICATES
UNIVERSITY OF TENNESSEE-CHATTANOOGA—TN	X	X	X	X		X		X	X	
UNIVERSITY OF TENNESSEE-MARTIN—TN	X	X	X			X		X		
UNIVERSITY OF WEST ALABAMA—AL	X	X	X	X	X			X		
UNIVERSITY OF WISCONSIN-EAU CLAIRE—WI	X	X	X	X	X	X		X	X	
UNIVERSITY OF WISCONSIN-LA CROSSE—WI	X	X	X		X	X		X		
UNIVERSITY OF WISCONSIN-PLATTEVILLE—WI	X	X	X		X	X		X		
UNIVERSITY OF WISCONSIN-RIVER FALLS—WI	X	X	X	X	X	X	X	X	X	
UNIVERSITY OF WISCONSIN-STEVENS POINT—WI	X	X	X		X	X	X	X	X	
UNIVERSITY OF WISCONSIN-STOUT—WI	X	X	X	X	X	X	X	X	X	X
UNIVERSITY OF WISCONSIN-SUPERIOR—WI	X	X	X		X	X	X	X	X	
UNIVERSITY OF WISCONSIN-WHITEWATER—WI	X	X	X		X	X				
VILLANOVA UNIVERSITY—PA	X	X	X	X		X				
WASHBURN UNIVERSITY OF TOPEKA—KS	X		X			X		X		
WEBSTER UNIVERSITY—MO	X	X	X	X	X		X	X	X	
WEST TEXAS A & M UNIVERSITY—TX	X	X	X			X		X		
WESTERN CAROLINA UNIVERSITY—NC	X	X	X		X	X	X	X	X	
WESTERN CONNECTICUT STATE UNIVERSITY—CT	X		X	X	X		X	X	X	
WESTERN ILLINOIS UNIVERSITY—IL	X		X	X	X	X		X	X	X
WESTERN KENTUCKY UNIVERSITY—KY	X	X	X	X	X	X				

INSTITUTION	ANY PRIOR LEARNING ASSESSMENT	ADVANCED PLACEMENT	CLEP	ACT/PEP	DANTES	CHALLENGE EXAM	ACE/ PONSI	ACE/MILITARY	INDIVIDUAL ASSESSMENT	ASSESSMENT OF CERTIFICATES
WESTERN NEW MEXICO UNIVERSITY—NM	X	X	X	X	X	X		X	X	
WESTERN OREGON STATE COLLEGE—OR	X	X	X		X	X	X	X		
WESTERN WASHINGTON UNIVERSITY—WA	X	X				X		X		
WIDENER UNIVERSITY-MAIN CAMPUS—PA	X	X	X		X	X	X	X	X	
WILLIAM PATERSON COLLEGE OF NEW JERSEY—NJ	X	X	X			X		X		
XAVIER UNIVERSITY—OH	X	X	X	X			X	X		X
MASTER'S (COMPREHENSIVE) UNIVERSITIES AND COLLEGES II										
BELMONT UNIVERSITY—TN	X	X	X		X	X	X	X		
CABRINI COLLEGE—PA	X	X	X	X	X	X	X	X	X	X
CALVIN COLLEGE—MI	X		X		X			X	X	X
CAPITAL UNIVERSITY—OH	X	X	X	X	X	X	X	X	X	X
CARTHAGE COLLEGE—WI	X	X	X		X	X		X		
CHESTNUT HILL COLLEGE—PA	X	X	X			X				
COLLEGE MISERICORDIA—PA	X	X	X	X				X	X	
COLLEGE OF NOTRE DAME MARYLAND—MD	X	X	X	X	X	X	X	X	X	
COLLEGE OF SAINT CATHERINE- SAINT CATHERINE CAMPUS—MN	X	X	X	X			X	X	X	X
COLORADO CHRISTIAN UNIVERSITY—CO	X	X	X	X	X	X	X	X	X	X
CORNERSTONE COLLEGE—MI	X	X	X		X			X	X	X

INSTITUTION	ANY PRIOR LEARNING ASSESSMENT	ADVANCED PLACEMENT	CLEP	ACT/PEP	DANTES	CHALLENGE EXAM	ACE/ PONSI	ACE/MILITARY	INDIVIDUAL ASSESSMENT	ASSESSMENT OF CERTIFICATES
CUMBERLAND COLLEGE—KY	X	X	X		X	X		X		
D'YOUVILLE COLLEGE—NY	X	X	X	X	X	X	X	X	X	
EASTERN COLLEGE—PA	X	X	X	X	X		X	X	X	X
FERRIS STATE UNIVERSITY—MI	X	X	X		X	X		X	X	
GWYNEDD-MERCY COLLEGE—PA	X	X	X	X	X	X		X	X	X
LAKE ERIE COLLEGE—OH	X	X	X		X		X	X	X	
LAKE SUPERIOR STATE UNIVERSITY—MI	X	X	X		X	X		X		
LENOIR-RHYNE COLLEGE—NC	X	X	X	X	X	X	X	X		X
LINCOLN UNIVERSITY—PA										
LINFIELD COLLEGE—OR	X	X	X		X	X	X	X	X	
MARIAN COLLEGE OF FOND DU LAC—WI	X	X	X	X	X	X	X	X	X	
MARYLHURST COLLEGE—OR	X	X	X	X	X	X	X	X	X	
MIDAMERICA NAZARENE COLLEGE—KS	X	X	X	X	X	X	X	X	X	
MONTANA TECH OF THE UNIVERSITY OF MONTANA—MT	X	X	X		X	X	X	X		
MOUNT SAINT MARY COLLEGE—NY	X	X	X	X	X	X	X	X	X	
MOUNT SAINT MARY'S COLLEGE—MD	X	X	X		X		X	X	X	
MOUNT SAINT MARY'S COLLEGE—CA										
NORTH CENTRAL COLLEGE—IL	X	X	X			X			X	
PACIFIC UNIVERSITY—OR	X	X	X			X				

INSTITUTION	ANY PRIOR LEARNING ASSESSMENT	ADVANCED PLACEMENT	CLEP	ACT/PEP	DANTES	CHALLENGE EXAM	ACE/PONSI	ACE/MILITARY	INDIVIDUAL ASSESSMENT	ASSESSMENT OF CERTIFICATES
PARK COLLEGE—MO	X	X	X	X	X		X	X	X	X
PFEIFFER COLLEGE—NC	X	X	X		X	X	X	X	X	
QUINNIPIAC COLLEGE—CT	X	X	X			X	X		X	
SAINT EDWARD'S UNIVERSITY—TX	X	X	X	X	X	X	X		X	
ST. JOHN FISHER COLLEGE—NY	X	X	X	X	X	X	X	X		
SOUTHERN ARKANSAS UNIVERSITY MAIN CAMPUS—AR	X	X	X			X	X	X	X	
SOUTHWEST BAPTIST UNIVERSITY—MO	X	X	X		X			X	X	
SPRING HILL COLLEGE—AL	X	X	X					X	X	
TEIKYO MARYCREST UNIVERSITY—IA	X	X	X	X	X	X		X	X	
THE UNIVERSITY OF CHARLESTON—VA	X	X	X		X	X	X	X	X	X
TUSCULUM COLLEGE—TN	X	X	X	X			X	X	X	
UNION COLLEGE—KY	X	X	X			X		X	X	
UNIVERSIDADMETROPOLITANA—PR	X	X	X			X		X		
UNIVERSITY OF SACRED HEART—PR	X	X				X		X	X	
UNIVERSITY OF SOUTHERN INDIANA—IN	X	X	X		X	X		X		X
UNIVERSITY OF TAMPA—FL	X	X	X	X	X	X	X	X	X	X
UNIVERSITY OF WISCONSIN-PARKSIDE—WI	X	X	X		X	X		X		
VITERBO COLLEGE—WI	X	X	X		X	X		X	X	

INSTITUTION	ANY PRIOR LEARNING ASSESSMENT	ADVANCED PLACEMENT	CLEP	ACT/PEP	DANTES	CHALLENGE EXAM	ACE/PONSI	ACE/MILITARY	INDIVIDUAL ASSESSMENT	ASSESSMENT OF CERTIFICATES
WALLA WALLA COLLEGE—WA	X	X	X			X				
WALSH UNIVERSITY—OH	X	X	X		X		X	X	X	
WEBER STATE UNIVERSITY—UT	X	X	X			X		X		
BACCALAUREATE (LIBERAL ARTS) COLLEGES I										
AGNES SCOTT COLLEGE—GA	X	X								
ALBION COLLEGE—MI	X	X	X							
ALBRIGHT COLLEGE—PA	X	X	X			X			X	
AMHERST COLLEGE—MA										
AUGUSTANA COLLEGE—IL	X	X			X	X		X		
BARNARD COLLEGE—NY	X	X								
BELOIT COLLEGE—WI	X	X	X	X	X	X		X	X	
BIRMINGHAM SOUTHERN COLLEGE—AL	X	X	X			X			X	
BRYN MAWR COLLEGE—PA	X	X								
BUCKNELL UNIVERSITY—PA	X	X	X			X				
CENTRAL COLLEGE—IA	X	X	X	X	X	X	X	X		
COE COLLEGE—IA	X	X	X	X				X		
COLBY COLLEGE—ME										
COLGATE UNIVERSITY—NY	X	X	X							
COLLEGE OF SAINT BENEDICT—MN	X	X	X			X		X		

INSTITUTION	ANY PRIOR LEARNING ASSESSMENT	ADVANCED PLACEMENT	CLEP	ACT/PEP	DANTES	CHALLENGE EXAM	ACE/ PONSI	ACE/MILITARY	INDIVIDUAL ASSESSMENT	ASSESSMENT OF CERTIFICATES
COLLEGE OF WOOSTER—OH	X	X						X		
COLORADO COLLEGE—CO	X	X								
CONCORDIA COLLEGE AT MOORHEAD—MN	X		X		X	X	X	X	X	X
CONNECTICUT COLLEGE—CT	X	X						X		
CORNELL COLLEGE—IA	X	X	X			X				
DENISON UNIVERSITY—OH	X	X								
DEPAUW UNIVERSITY—IN	X	X							X	
DICKINSON COLLEGE—PA	X	X								
EARLHAM COLLEGE—IN	X	X								
FRANKLIN AND MARSHALL COLLEGE—PA	X		X			X				
FRANKLIN COLLEGE OF INDIANA—IN	X	X	X		X			X		
FURMAN UNIVERSITY—SC	X	X	X			X				
GEORGETOWN COLLEGE—KY	X	X	X							
GORDON COLLEGE—MA										
GOSHEN COLLEGE—IN	X	X	X		X	X	X	X	X	X
GRINNELL COLLEGE—IA	X	X								
GUILFORD COLLEGE—NC	X	X	X		X					
GUSTAVUS ADOLPHUS COLLEGE—MN	X	X				X				
HAMILTON COLLEGE—NY	X	X								

INSTITUTION	ANY PRIOR LEARNING ASSESSMENT	ADVANCED PLACEMENT	CLEP	ACT/PEP	DANTES	CHALLENGE EXAM	ACE/PONSI	ACE/MILITARY	INDIVIDUAL ASSESSMENT	ASSESSMENT OF CERTIFICATES
HAMLINE UNIVERSITY—MN	X	X	X		X	X		X		
HAMPDEN-SYDNEY COLLEGE—VA	X	X								
HARTWICK COLLEGE—NY	X	X	X	X	X	X	X	X	X	
HAVERFORD COLLEGE—PA	X	X								
HENDRIX COLLEGE—AR	X	X	X			X				
HIRAM COLLEGE—OH	X	X	X	X			X	X	X	
HOLLINS COLLEGE—VA	X	X								
HOUGHTON COLLEGE—NY	X	X	X	X	X	X	X	X	X	X
ILLINOIS COLLEGE—IL	X	X	X			X		X		
ILLINOIS WESLEYAN UNIVERSITY—IL	X	X	X							
KENYON COLLEGE—OH	X	X								
LAFAYETTE COLLEGE—PA										
LAKE FOREST COLLEGE—IL	X	X								
LAWRENCE UNIVERSITY—WI	X	X				X				
LEWIS AND CLARK COLLEGE—OR										
MACALESTER COLLEGE—MN	X	X								
MARLBORO COLLEGE—VT	X	X	X		X					
MONMOUTH COLLEGE—IL	X	X						X		
MORAVIAN COLLEGE—PA	X	X	X		X	X				

INSTITUTION	ANY PRIOR LEARNING ASSESSMENT	ADVANCED PLACEMENT	CLEP	ACT/PEP	DANTES	CHALLENGE EXAM	ACE/ PONSI	ACE/MILITARY	INDIVIDUAL ASSESSMENT	ASSESSMENT OF CERTIFICATES
MOUNT HOLYOKE COLLEGE—MA	X	X								
MUHLENBERG COLLEGE—PA	X		X		X		X		X	
NEBRASKA WESLEYAN UNIVERSITY—NE	X	X	X	X		X	X	X		
OGLETHORPE UNIVERSITY—GA	X	X	X		X	X	X	X	X	
OHIO WESLEYAN UNIVERSITY—OH	X	X				X		X		
PITZER COLLEGE—CA	X	X							X	
RHODES COLLEGE—TN										
RIPON COLLEGE—WI	X	X						X		
SAINT JOHN'S UNIVERSITY—MN	X	X	X			X		X		
ST. MARY'S COLLEGE OF MARYLAND—MD	X	X	X		X		X	X		
SALEM COLLEGE—NC	X	X	X					X	X	
SARAH LAWRENCE COLLEGE—NY	X	X							X	
SCRIPP'S COLLEGE—CA	X	X	X							
SHEPHERD COLLEGE—WV	X	X	X		X	X		X	X	X
SIENA COLLEGE—NY	X	X	X						X	
SMITH COLLEGE—MA	X	X								
SOUTHWESTERN UNIVERSITY—TX	X	X				X		X		
SPELMAN COLLEGE—GA	X	X	X						X	
ST. JOHN'S COLLEGE—MD										

INSTITUTION	ANY PRIOR LEARNING ASSESSMENT	ADVANCED PLACEMENT	CLEP	ACT/PEP	DANTES	CHALLENGE EXAM	ACE/PONSI	ACE/MILITARY	INDIVIDUAL ASSESSMENT	ASSESSMENT OF CERTIFICATES
ST. JOHN'S COLLEGE—NM										
ST. LAWRENCE UNIVERSITY—NY	X	X	X	X						
SWARTHMORE COLLEGE—PA	X	X								
SWEET BRIAR COLLEGE—VA	X	X								
THE RICHARD STOCKTON COLLEGE OF NEW JERSEY—NJ	X	X	X	X	X			X		
TRINITY COLLEGE—CT	X	X				X				
UNIVERSITY OF JUDAISM—CA	X					X				
UNIVERSITY OF NORTH CAROLINA AT ASHEVILLE—NC	X	X	X	X	X	X				
UNIVERSITY OF PUERTO RICO-CAYEY UNIVERSITY COLLEGE—PR	X	X								
UNIVERSITY OF PUGET SOUND—WA										
VIRGINIA MILITARY INSTITUTE—VA	X	X				X		X		
WABASH COLLEGE—IN	X	X	X							
WARTBURG COLLEGE—IA	X	X	X			X	X	X	X	
WASHINGTON AND JEFFERSON COLLEGE—PA	X	X	X					X		
WASHINGTON AND LEE UNIVERSITY—KY	X	X				X				
WASHINGTON COLLEGE—MD	X									
WELLESLEY COLLEGE—MA	X	X								
WELLS COLLEGE—NY	X	X	X			X			X	

INSTITUTION	ANY PRIOR LEARNING ASSESSMENT	ADVANCED PLACEMENT	CLEP	ACT/PEP	DANTES	CHALLENGE EXAM	ACE/PONSI	ACE/MILITARY	INDIVIDUAL ASSESSMENT	ASSESSMENT OF CERTIFICATES
WESLEYAN COLLEGE—GA	X	X	X			X	X	X	X	
WESTERN MARYLAND COLLEGE—MD	X	X	X					X		
WESTMONT COLLEGE—CA	X	X	X			X		X		
WHEATON COLLEGE—IL	X	X	X			X		X		
WHITMAN COLLEGE—WA	X					X		X		
WILLIAM JEWELL COLLEGE—MO	X	X	X	X	X	X	X	X		
WITTENBERG UNIVERSITY—OH	X	X	X			X				
WOFFORD COLLEGE—SC	X	X	X		X			X		
BACCALAUREATE COLLEGES II										
ALLENTOWN COLLEGE OF SAINT FRANCIS DE SALES—PA	X	X	X		X	X		X	X	
ALVERNIA COLLEGE—PA	X	X	X	X	X	X	X	X	X	
ALVERNO COLLEGE—WI	X	X	X			X			X	
AMBASSADOR UNIVERSITY—TX	X	X	X					X		
AUGUSTANA COLLEGE—SD	X	X	X	X	X	X		X	X	
BARAT COLLEGE—IL	X	X	X		X				X	
BELHAVEN COLLEGE—MS	X	X	X		X	X	X		X	
BENEDICTINE COLLEGE—KS	X	X	X	X	X	X		X	X	
BETHANY COLLEGE OF THE ASSEMBLIES OF GOD—CA	X	X	X		X	X		X	X	
BETHEL COLLEGE—TN	X	X	X		X		X	X	X	

INSTITUTION	ANY PRIOR LEARNING ASSESSMENT	ADVANCED PLACEMENT	CLEP	ACT/PEP	DANTES	CHALLENGE EXAM	ACE/ PONSI	ACE/MILITARY	INDIVIDUAL ASSESSMENT	ASSESSMENT OF CERTIFICATES
BETHEL COLLEGE—KS	X	X	X			X		X	X	
BETHEL COLLEGE—MN	X	X	X	X	X	X	X	X	X	X
BETHEL COLLEGE—IN	X	X	X	X	X	X	X	X	X	X
BETHUNE COOKMAN COLLEGE—FL	X	X	X		X	X		X		
BLUE MOUNTAIN COLLEGE—MS	X	X	X						X	
BLUEFIELD COLLEGE—VA	X	X	X		X		X	X	X	X
BLUEFIELD STATE COLLEGE—WV	X	X	X			X		X	X	X
BLUFFTON COLLEGE—OH	X	X	X	X	X	X	X	X	X	
BRADFORD COLLEGE—MA	X	X	X		X		X	X		
BRESCIA COLLEGE—KY	X	X	X			X	X	X	X	
BREWTON-PARKER COLLEGE—GA	X	X	X							
BRIDGEWATER COLLEGE—VA	X	X							X	
BUENA VISTA UNIVERSITY—IA	X	X	X		X		X	X	X	
CALUMET COLLEGE OF SAINT JOSEPH—IN	X		X		X	X	X	X	X	
CAMERON UNIVERSITY—OK	X	X	X	X	X	X		X		
CARLOW COLLEGE—PA	X	X	X	X		X	X	X	X	
CARROLL COLLEGE—MT	X	X	X			X		X		
CARROLL COLLEGE—WI	X	X	X	X		X				
CARSON-NEWMAN COLLEGE—TN	X	X	X	X	X	X		X	X	

INSTITUTION	ANY PRIOR LEARNING ASSESSMENT	ADVANCED PLACEMENT	CLEP	ACT/PEP	DANTES	CHALLENGE EXAM	ACE/ PONSI	ACE/MILITARY	INDIVIDUAL ASSESSMENT	ASSESSMENT OF CERTIFICATES
CATAWBA COLLEGE—NC	X	X				X		X		
CENTRAL METHODIST COLLEGE—MO	X	X	X		X	X				
CHARTER OAK STATE COLLEGE—CT	X		X	X	X		X	X	X	X
CHRISTIAN HERITAGE COLLEGE—CA	X	X	X	X	X		X	X	X	
CHRISTOPHER NEWPORT UNIVERSITY—VA	X	X	X		X	X	X	X		
CLARKE COLLEGE—IA	X	X	X	X	X		X	X	X	
CLEARWATER CHRISTIAN COLLEGE—FL	X	X	X					X		
COKER COLLEGE—SC	X	X	X		X	X	X	X	X	
COLLEGE FOR LIFELONG LEARNING—NH	X	X	X	X				X	X	
COLLEGE OF MOUNT SAINT VINCENT—NY	X		X		X	X		X		
COLLEGE OF OUR LADY OF THE ELMS—MA	X	X	X		X	X		X	X	X
COLLEGE OF SAINT ELIZABETH—NJ	X	X	X	X	X			X	X	
COLLEGE OF SAINT JOSEPH—VT	X	X	X				X	X	X	X
COLLEGE OF SAINT MARY—NE	X		X	X	X	X	X	X	X	
COLLEGE OF SANTA FE—NM	X	X	X	X	X	X	X	X	X	
COLLEGE OF THE OZARKS—MO	X	X	X			X		X		
COLLEGE OF THE SOUTHWEST—NM	X	X	X	X	X	X	X	X	X	
COLUMBIA COLLEGE—SC	X	X	X			X			X	
COLUMBIA COLLEGE—IL	X	X	X		X				X	

INSTITUTION	ANY PRIOR LEARNING ASSESSMENT	ADVANCED PLACEMENT	CLEP	ACT/PEP	DANTES	CHALLENGE EXAM	ACE/ PONSI	ACE/MILITARY	INDIVIDUAL ASSESSMENT	ASSESSMENT OF CERTIFICATES
COLUMBIA UNION COLLEGE—MD	X	X	X	X	X	X	X	X	X	X
CONCORDIA COLLEGE—NY	X	X	X	X	X	X	X	X	X	
CONCORDIA COLLEGE—MN	X	X	X	X	X	X	X	X	X	X
CONCORDIA COLLEGE—MI	X	X	X	X		X	X	X	X	X
CONCORDIA UNIVERSITY—OR	X	X	X		X	X	X	X	X	X
CONCORDIA UNIVERSITY-WISCONSIN—WI	X	X	X	X	X	X	X	X	X	
COVENANT COLLEGE—GA	X	X	X		X		X	X	X	
CULVER-STOCKTON COLLEGE—MO	X	X	X	X	X	X			X	
CUMBERLAND UNIVERSITY—TN	X	X	X	X	X		X	X	X	
DAEMEN COLLEGE—NY	X		X	X	X	X	X	X	X	
DAKOTA STATE UNIVERSITY—SD	X	X	X		X	X	X	X	X	
DAVIS AND ELKINS COLLEGE—WV	X	X	X	X	X	X	X	X	X	X
DELAWARE VALLEY COLLEGE—PA	X	X	X			X		X		
DICKINSON STATE UNIVERSITY—ND	X	X	X		X	X		X	X	
DIVINE WORD COLLEGE—IA	X	X	X			X				
DOMINICAN COLLEGE OF BLAUVELT—NY	X	X	X			X	X	X	X	
DORDT COLLEGE—IA	X	X	X		X		X	X		
EASTERN MENNONITE UNIVERSITY—VA	X	X	X		X	X		X		
EASTERN OREGON STATE COLLEGE—OR	X	X	X			X		X	X	

INSTITUTION	ANY PRIOR LEARNING ASSESSMENT	ADVANCED PLACEMENT	CLEP	ACT/PEP	DANTES	CHALLENGE EXAM	ACE/PONSI	ACE/MILITARY	INDIVIDUAL ASSESSMENT	ASSESSMENT OF CERTIFICATES
ELIZABETH CITY STATE UNIVERSITY—NC	X	X	X					X		
ELIZABETHTOWN COLLEGE—PA	X		X		X	X	X	X	X	
ELMHURST COLLEGE—IL	X	X	X					X	X	X
EMORY AND HENRY COLLEGE—VA										X
EUREKA COLLEGE—IL	X	X	X		X					
FAIRMONT STATE COLLEGE—WV	X	X	X		X	X	X	X	X	X
FAULKNER UNIVERSITY—AL	X	X	X		X		X	X		X
FLORIDA SOUTHERN COLLEGE—FL	X		X		X		X	X		
FRANKLIN PIERCE COLLEGE—NH	X	X	X		X		X	X	X	X
FREED-HARDEMAN UNIVERSITY—TN	X	X	X		X	X		X		
GENEVA COLLEGE—PA	X	X	X	X	X	X	X	X	X	X
GRACE COLLEGE AND THEOLOGICAL SEMINARY—IN	X	X	X	X	X	X	X	X	X	
GRACELAND COLLEGE—IA	X	X	X	X	X	X	X	X	X	
GREEN MOUNTAIN COLLEGE—VT	X	X	X	X	X	X	X	X	X	
GREENSBORO COLLEGE—NC	X	X	X	X	X	X		X	X	
GREENVILLE COLLEGE—IL	X	X	X		X	X	X	X	X	
HANNIBAL-LAGRANGE COLLEGE—MO	X		X	X	X	X		X	X	
HEIDELBERG COLLEGE—OH	X	X	X	X	X	X	X	X	X	
HIGH POINT UNIVERSITY—NC	X	X	X		X	X	X	X	X	

INSTITUTION	ANY PRIOR LEARNING ASSESSMENT	ADVANCED PLACEMENT	CLEP	ACT/PEP	DANTES	CHALLENGE EXAM	ACE/ PONSI	ACE/MILITARY	INDIVIDUAL ASSESSMENT	ASSESSMENT OF CERTIFICATES
HILBERT COLLEGE—NY	X	X	X	X	X		X	X		
HILLSDALE COLLEGE—MI	X	X	X							
HOLY FAMILY COLLEGE—PA	X	X	X		X	X	X	X		
HOWARD PAYNE UNIVERSITY—TX	X	X	X	X	X	X	X	X	X	
HUNTINGTON COLLEGE—IN	X	X	X	X	X		X	X	X	X
HURON UNIVERSITY—SD	X	X	X	X	X	X		X	X	
INDIANA UNIVERSITY-EAST—IN	X	X	X		X		X	X	X	
JAMESTOWN COLLEGE—ND	X	X	X	X	X	X		X	X	
JARVIS CHRISTIAN COLLEGE—TX	X	X	X							
JOHN BROWN UNIVERSITY—AR	X		X		X		X	X	X	X
JOHNSON C. SMITH UNIVERSITY—NC	X	X		X						
KANSAS NEWMAN COLLEGE—KS	X	X	X	X	X	X	X	X	X	X
KENDALL COLLEGE—IL	X	X	X	X	X	X	X	X	X	
KEUKA COLLEGE—NY	X	X	X	X	X	X	X	X	X	
KING COLLEGE—TN	X	X	X					X		
KING'S COLLEGE—PA	X	X	X	X				X		
LAMBUTH UNIVERSITY—TN	X	X	X	X	X		X	X		
LANE COLLEGE—TN	X	X	X					X		
LAWRENCE TECHNOLOGICAL UNIVERSITY—MI	X	X	X	X	X			X		

INSTITUTION	ANY PRIOR LEARNING ASSESSMENT	ADVANCED PLACEMENT	CLEP	ACT/PEP	DANTES	CHALLENGE EXAM	ACE/PONSI	ACE/MILITARY	INDIVIDUAL ASSESSMENT	ASSESSMENT OF CERTIFICATES
LEBANON VALLEY COLLEGE—PA	X		X	X	X	X	X	X	X	
LEE COLLEGE—TN	X	X	X		X	X		X		
LETOURNEAU UNIVERSITY—TX	X	X	X	X	X		X	X	X	X
LEWIS-CLARK STATE COLLEGE—ID	X	X	X	X	X	X	X	X	X	
LIMESTONE COLLEGE—SC	X	X	X		X	X	X	X		
LINDSEY WILSON COLLEGE—KY	X	X	X		X	X		X		
LORAS COLLEGE—IA	X		X		X	X	X	X	X	
LOUISIANA COLLEGE—LA	X		X			X		X		
LOURDES COLLEGE—OH	X	X	X	X		X	X	X	X	X
LYCOMING COLLEGE—PA	X	X	X	X	X	X				
LYNDON STATE COLLEGE—VT	X	X	X	X	X	X	X	X	X	
MACMURRAY COLLEGE—IL	X	X	X		X		X	X		
MANCHESTER COLLEGE—IN	X	X								
MARIETTA COLLEGE—OH	X	X	X		X	X	X	X	X	
MARS HILL COLLEGE—NC	X		X		X	X		X	X	
MARTIN UNIVERSITY—IN	X		X		X			X	X	X
MARYMOUNT COLLEGE—NY	X	X	X						X	
MARYMOUNT MANHATTAN COLLEGE—NY	X	X	X		X		X	X	X	
MCKENDREE COLLEGE—IL	X	X	X	X	X	X		X		

INSTITUTION	ANY PRIOR LEARNING ASSESSMENT	ADVANCED PLACEMENT	CLEP	ACT/PEP	DANTES	CHALLENGE EXAM	ACE/ PONSI	ACE/MILITARY	INDIVIDUAL ASSESSMENT	ASSESSMENT OF CERTIFICATES
MCMURRY UNIVERSITY—TX	X	X	X	X	X	X		X		
METHODIST COLLEGE—NC	X	X	X		X	X		X		
METROPOLITAN STATE COLLEGE OF DENVER—CO	X	X	X	X	X	X	X	X	X	X
MIDLAND LUTHERAN COLLEGE—NE	X	X	X	X	X	X	X	X		
MILLIGAN COLLEGE—TN	X	X	X	X	X		X	X	X	X
MISSISSIPPI UNIVERSITY FOR WOMEN—MS	X	X	X		X	X	X	X		
MISSOURI SOUTHERN STATE COLLEGE—MO	X	X	X			X		X		
MISSOURI VALLEY COLLEGE—MO	X	X	X	X	X		X	X		
MOLLOY COLLEGE—NY	X	X	X	X	X	X	X	X	X	X
MORNINGSIDE COLLEGE—IA	X	X	X		X		X	X	X	
MOUNT MARY COLLEGE—WI	X	X	X		X	X	X	X	X	
MOUNT MERCY COLLEGE—IA	X	X	X	X	X			X	X	
MOUNT SENARIO COLLEGE—WI	X	X	X	X	X	X	X	X	X	
MOUNT ST. CLARE COLLEGE—IA	X	X	X			X		X		
MOUNT UNION COLLEGE—OH	X	X	X						X	X
MOUNT VERNON COLLEGE—DC	X	X	X		X	X		X	X	
MOUNT VERNON NAZARENE COLLEGE—OH	X	X	X			X		X	X	
MUSKINGUM COLLEGE—OH	X	X	X	X	X	X	X	X	X	
NEUMANN COLLEGE—PA	X	X	X	X	X	X	X	X	X	

INSTITUTION	ANY PRIOR LEARNING ASSESSMENT	ADVANCED PLACEMENT	CLEP	ACT/PEP	DANTES	CHALLENGE EXAM	ACE/ PONSI	ACE/MILITARY	INDIVIDUAL ASSESSMENT	ASSESSMENT OF CERTIFICATES
NEW COLLEGE OF CALIFORNIA—CA	X		X		X				X	
NEW ENGLAND COLLEGE—NH	X	X	X		X		X	X	X	
NEWBERRY COLLEGE—SC	X	X	X		X			X		
NORTH PARK COLLEGE AND THEOLOGICAL SEMINARY—IL	X	X	X	X	X	X		X	X	
NORTHLAND COLLEGE—WI	X	X	X		X	X	X	X	X	
NORTHWEST CHRISTIAN COLLEGE—OR	X	X	X		X	X	X	X	X	
NORTHWEST NAZARENE COLLEGE—ID	X	X	X			X				
NORTHWESTERN COLLEGE—IA	X	X	X		X			X		
OAKWOOD COLLEGE—AL	X	X	X		X	X		X	X	X
OHIO DOMINICAN COLLEGE—OH	X	X	X	X	X	X	X	X	X	
OTTAWA UNIVERSITY—KS	X	X	X	X	X		X	X	X	X
OUR LADY OF HOLY CROSS COLLEGE—LA	X	X	X	X	X	X	X	X	X	
PALM BEACH ATLANTIC COLLEGE—FL	X	X	X					X	X	X
PERU STATE COLLEGE—NE	X	X	X	X	X	X	X	X	X	
PIEDMONT COLLEGE—GA	X	X	X		X			X	X	
PINE MANOR COLLEGE—MA	X	X	X				X	X	X	
POINT PARK COLLEGE—PA	X	X	X		X	X	X	X	X	X
PRESCOTT COLLEGE—AZ	X	X	X		X	X			X	
PURDUE UNIVERSITY-NORTHCENTRAL CAMPUS—IN	X	X	X		X	X				

INSTITUTION	ANY PRIOR LEARNING ASSESSMENT	ADVANCED PLACEMENT	CLEP	ACT/PEP	DANTES	CHALLENGE EXAM	ACE/ PONSI	ACE/MILITARY	INDIVIDUAL ASSESSMENT	ASSESSMENT OF CERTIFICATES
QUINCY UNIVERSITY—IL	X	X	X			X		X	X	
RAMAPO COLLEGE OF NEW JERSEY—NJ	X	X	X	X	X		X	X	X	
ROBERTS WESLEYAN COLLEGE—NY	X	X	X	X	X		X	X	X	X
ROCKY MOUNTAIN COLLEGE—MT	X	X	X		X	X		X	X	X
ROSEMONT COLLEGE—PA	X	X	X		X		X	X	X	
SAINT JOSEPH'S COLLEGE—ME	X	X	X	X	X	X	X	X	X	
SAINT JOSEPH'S COLLEGE—IN	X	X	X				X	X	X	
SAINT MARY COLLEGE—KS	X	X	X	X	X	X	X	X	X	
SAINT MARY-OF-THE-WOODS COLLEGE—IN	X	X	X	X	X	X	X	X	X	X
SAINT MARY'S COLLEGE—IN	X	X	X							
SAINT MARY'S COLLEGE—MI	X	X	X			X	X		X	
SAINT MEINRAD COLLEGE—IN	X	X	X					X		
SAINT NORBERT COLLEGE—WI	X	X	X	X	X		X	X	X	
ST. THOMAS AQUINAS COLLEGE—NY	X	X	X		X		X	X	X	
SAINT VINCENT COLLEGE—PA	X	X	X		X	X		X	X	
SCHREINER COLLEGE—TX										
SHAWNEE STATE UNIVERSITY—OH	X	X	X	X	X	X		X		
SHELDON JACKSON COLLEGE—AK	X	X	X		X	X	X	X	X	
SIERRA NEVADA COLLEGE—NV	X	X	X			X		X	X	

INSTITUTION	ANY PRIOR LEARNING ASSESSMENT	ADVANCED PLACEMENT	CLEP	ACT/PEP	DANTES	CHALLENGE EXAM	ACE/ PONSI	ACE/MILITARY	INDIVIDUAL ASSESSMENT	ASSESSMENT OF CERTIFICATES
SILVER LAKE COLLEGE—WI	X	X	X				X	X	X	
SIMPSON COLLEGE—IA	X	X	X		X	X		X	X	X
SIMPSON COLLEGE—CA	X	X	X		X	X				
SOUTHERN CALIFORNIA COLLEGE—CA	X	X	X		X	X		X	X	X
SOUTHERN COLLEGE OF SEVENTH-DAY ADVENTISTS—TN	X	X	X			X		X		
SOUTHERN UTAH UNIVERSITY—UT	X	X	X			X		X		
SOUTHWESTERN COLLEGE—KS										
SPRING ARBOR COLLEGE—MI	X	X	X		X	X	X	X	X	X
STEPHENS COLLEGE—MO	X	X	X	X	X	X	X	X	X	
STONEHILL COLLEGE—MA	X	X	X							
SUNY COLLEGE AT OLD WESTBURY—NY	X	X	X		X				X	
SUNY COLLEGE AT PURCHASE—NY	X	X	X				X	X	X	
SUSQUEHANNA UNIVERSITY—PA	X	X	X						X	
TABOR COLLEGE—KS	X	X	X	X	X	X	X	X	X	X
TENNESSEE WESLEYAN COLLEGE—TN	X	X	X		X	X	X	X		
TEXAS LUTHERAN COLLEGE—TX	X	X	X	X	X	X		X		
THE MASTERS COLLEGE—CA	X	X	X					X	X	
THIEL COLLEGE—PA	X	X	X	X	X			X	X	

INSTITUTION	ANY PRIOR LEARNING ASSESSMENT	ADVANCED PLACEMENT	CLEP	ACT/PEP	DANTES	CHALLENGE EXAM	ACE/ PONSI	ACE/MILITARY	INDIVIDUAL ASSESSMENT	ASSESSMENT OF CERTIFICATES
THOMAS A. EDISON STATE COLLEGE—NJ	X		X	X	X	X	X	X	X	X
THOMAS MORE COLLEGE—KY	X	X	X	X	X	X	X	X	X	X
TOCCOA FALLS COLLEGE—GA	X	X	X		X		X	X		
TRI-STATE UNIVERSITY—IN	X	X	X		X	X	X	X		
TRINITY CHRISTIAN COLLEGE—IL	X	X	X	X		X				
TRINITY COLLEGE OF VERMONT—VT	X	X	X	X	X		X	X	X	
UNION COLLEGE—NE										
UNIVERSITY OF ARKANSAS AT MONTICELLO—AR										
UNIVERSITY OF HAWAII AT WEST OAHU—HI										
UNIVERSITY OF MAINE AT FARMINGTON—ME	X	X	X		X	X		X		X
UNIVERSITY OF MAINE AT FORT KENT—ME	X	X	X	X	X		X	X	X	
UNIVERSITY OF PUERTO RICO-HUMACAO UNIVERSITY COLLEGE—PR	X	X				X				
UNIVERSITY OF SIOUX FALLS—SD	X	X	X		X	X	X	X	X	
UNIVERSITY OF SOUTH CAROLINA AT SPARTANBURG—SC	X	X	X	X	X	X		X		
UNIVERSITY OF VIRGINIA-CLINCH VALLEY COLLEGE—VA	X	X				X		X		
URSULINE COLLEGE—OH	X	X	X			X		X	X	X
UTICA COLLEGE OF SYRACUSE UNIVERSITY—NY	X	X	X	X	X	X	X	X	X	
VALLEY CITY STATE UNIVERSITY—ND	X	X	X		X	X		X	X	

INSTITUTION	ANY PRIOR LEARNING ASSESSMENT	ADVANCED PLACEMENT	CLEP	ACT/PEP	DANTES	CHALLENGE EXAM	ACE/PONSI	ACE/MILITARY	INDIVIDUAL ASSESSMENT	ASSESSMENT OF CERTIFICATES
WARNER PACIFIC COLLEGE—OR	X	X	X		X	X	X	X	X	X
WARNER SOUTHERN COLLEGE—FL	X	X	X		X		X	X	X	X
WAYLAND BAPTIST UNIVERSITY—TX	X	X	X	X	X	X	X	X	X	X
WAYNESBURG COLLEGE—PA	X		X	X	X	X	X	X	X	
WEST VIRGINIA STATE COLLEGE—WV	X	X	X	X	X	X	X	X	X	X
WESTERN BAPTIST COLLEGE—OR	X	X	X	X	X	X	X	X	X	
WESTERN MONTANA COLLEGE- UNIVERSITY OF MONTANA—MT	X	X	X			X		X		
WESTERN STATE COLLEGE COLORADO—CO	X	X	X		X		X	X		
WESTMAR UNIVERSITY—IA	X		X			X		X	X	X
WILLIAM WOODS UNIVERSITY—MO	X		X	X	X		X	X	X	
WILLIAMS BAPTIST COLLEGE—AR	X	X	X		X	X		X	X	
WINGATE UNIVERSITY—NC	X	X	X		X	X		X		
WINSTON-SALEM STATE UNIVERSITY—NC	X		X	X	X	X	X	X		X
WISCONSIN LUTHERAN COLLEGE—WI	X	X	X		X	X	X		X	
YORK COLLEGE PENNSYLVANIA—PA	X	X	X	X	X	X	X	X		
ASSOCIATE OF ARTS COLLEGES										
ABRAHAM BALDWIN AGRICULTURAL COLLEGE—GA	X	X	X		X	X	X	X		
AIKEN TECHNICAL COLLEGE—SC	X	X	X			X		X		

INSTITUTION	ANY PRIOR LEARNING ASSESSMENT	ADVANCED PLACEMENT	CLEP	ACT/PEP	DANTES	CHALLENGE EXAM	ACE/ PONSI	ACE/MILITARY	INDIVIDUAL ASSESSMENT	ASSESSMENT OF CERTIFICATES
AIMS COMMUNITY COLLEGE—CO	X	X	X	X	X	X	X	X	X	
ALLAN HANCOCK COLLEGE—CA	X	X	X		X	X		X		
ALVIN COMMUNITY COLLEGE—TX	X	X	X	X	X	X		X		X
AMERICAN ACADEMY MCALISTER INST OF FUNERAL SERVICE—NY										
ANCILLA COLLEGE—IN										
ANDREW COLLEGE—GA	X	X	X		X	X		X	X	
ANNE ARUNDEL COMMUNITY COLLEGE—MD	X	X	X		X	X	X	X		
AQUINAS COLLEGE—TN	X	X								
ASSUMPTION COLLEGE FOR SISTERS—NJ										
BACONE COLLEGE—OK	X	X	X			X		X		
BARTON COUNTY COMMUNITY COLLEGE—KS	X	X	X		X			X		
BAY PATH COLLEGE—MA	X	X	X							
BEAUFORT COUNTY COMMUNITY COLLEGE—DC	X	X	X		X	X				
BELLEVILLE AREA COLLEGE—IL	X	X	X		X			X	X	X
BERKSHIRE COMMUNITY COLLEGE—MA	X		X		X	X	X	X	X	X
BETHANY LUTHERAN COLLEGE—MN	X	X	X							
BIG BEND COMMUNITY COLLEGE—WA	X	X	X	X	X	X		X	X	
BLINN COLLEGE—TX	X		X					X		

INSTITUTION	ANY PRIOR LEARNING ASSESSMENT	ADVANCED PLACEMENT	CLEP	ACT/PEP	DANTES	CHALLENGE EXAM	ACE/PONSI	ACE/MILITARY	INDIVIDUAL ASSESSMENT	ASSESSMENT OF CERTIFICATES
BREVARD COMMUNITY COLLEGE—FL	X		X		X	X		X	X	X
BRIARWOOD COLLEGE—CT	X		X	X		X			X	
BRISTOL COMMUNITY COLLEGE—MA	X		X			X		X		
BROOME COMMUNITY COLLEGE—NY	X	X	X			X			X	
BRUNSWICK COLLEGE—GA	X	X	X		X			X	X	X
BUNKER HILL COMMUNITY COLLEGE—MA	X	X	X	X	X	X	X	X	X	X
BUTLER COUNTY COMMUNITY COLLEGE—KS	X	X	X	X	X	X	X	X		X
BUTLER COUNTY COMMUNITY COLLEGE—PA	X	X	X	X	X	X	X	X	X	
CARL SANDBURG COLLEGE—IL	X	X	X	X	X			X		
CARTERET COMMUNITY COLLEGE—NC	X	X	X		X	X	X	X		X
CAYUGA COUNTY COMMUNITY COLLEGE—NY	X	X	X		X	X	X	X		
CECIL COMMUNITY COLLEGE—MD	X	X	X	X	X	X		X	X	
CEDAR VALLEY COLLEGE—TX	X		X		X	X			X	
CENTRAL ARIZONA COLLEGE—AZ	X	X	X			X		X		
CENTRAL CAROLINA COMMUNITY COLLEGE—NC	X		X		X	X		X	X	
CENTRAL OHIO TECHNICAL COLLEGE—OH	X									
CENTRAL TEXAS COLLEGE—TX	X	X	X	X	X	X	X	X	X	X
CENTRAL VIRGINIA COMMUNITY COLLEGE—VA	X	X	X		X	X	X	X	X	X
CHEMEKETA COMMUNITY COLLEGE—OR	X	X	X		X	X		X	X	

INSTITUTION	ANY PRIOR LEARNING ASSESSMENT	ADVANCED PLACEMENT	CLEP	ACT/PEP	DANTES	CHALLENGE EXAM	ACE/PONSI	ACE/MILITARY	INDIVIDUAL ASSESSMENT	ASSESSMENT OF CERTIFICATES
CHIPOLA JUNIOR COLLEGE—FL	X	X	X							
CHIPPEWA VALLEY TECHNICAL COLLEGE—WI	X		X			X		X	X	
CHOWAN COLLEGE—NC	X	X	X	X	X	X	X	X	X	
CLARK STATE COMMUNITY COLLEGE—OH	X	X	X	X		X	X	X	X	
CLEVELAND STATE COMMUNITY COLLEGE—TN	X	X	X		X	X		X	X	X
CLINTON COMMUNITY COLLEGE—NY	X	X	X		X	X	X	X	X	
COASTAL CAROLINA COMMUNITY COLLEGE—NC	X	X	X		X	X	X	X		
COLBY COMMUNITY COLLEGE—KS	X		X			X		X	X	
COLLEGE OF EASTERN UTAH—UT	X		X		X	X		X		
COLLEGE OF THE ALBEMARLE—NC	X	X	X			X		X		
COLLIN COUNTY COMMUNITY COLLEGE-CENTRAL PARK—TX	X	X	X	X	X	X	X	X	X	
COLUMBIA JUNIOR COLLEGE OF BUSINESS—SC										
COLUMBUS STATE COMMUNITY COLLEGE—OH	X		X		X	X	X	X	X	X
COMMONWEALTH COLLEGE-VIRGINIA BEACH—VA	X	X	X		X	X		X		
COMMONWEALTH INSTITUTE OF FUNERAL SERVICE—TX	X		X							
CRAVEN COMMUNITY COLLEGE—NC	X	X	X		X	X		X		
CUNY LA GUARDIA COMMUNITY COLLEGE—NY	X	X		X	X	X	X	X	X	
CYPRESS COLLEGE—CA										
DAWSON COMMUNITY COLLEGE—MT	X	X	X		X	X		X	X	

INSTITUTION	ANY PRIOR LEARNING ASSESSMENT	ADVANCED PLACEMENT	CLEP	ACT/PEP	DANTES	CHALLENGE EXAM	ACE/ PONSI	ACE/MILITARY	INDIVIDUAL ASSESSMENT	ASSESSMENT OF CERTIFICATES
DELAWARE COUNTY COMMUNITY COLLEGE—PA	X	X	X	X	X	X		X	X	X
DELAWARE TECHNICAL AND COMMUNITY COLLEGE-TERRY—DE	X		X		X	X		X	X	
DELGADO COMMUNITY COLLEGE—LA	X	X	X			X		X	X	
DES MOINES COMMUNITY COLLEGE—IA	X	X	X	X	X	X	X	X		
DONNELLY COLLEGE—KS	X	X	X			X			X	
DRAUGHONS JUNIOR COLLEGE OF BUSINESS—TN										
DUNDALK COMMUNITY COLLEGE—MD	X	X	X	X	X	X	X	X	X	X
EAST CENTRAL COLLEGE—MO	X	X	X			X		X		
EASTFIELD COLLEGE—TX	X	X	X		X	X	X	X	X	
EL CENTRO COLLEGE—TX	X	X	X		X	X		X	X	
EMMANUEL COLLEGE—GA	X	X	X				X	X		
ERIE COMMUNITY COLLEGE-SOUTH CAMPUS—NY	X		X	X	X	X		X	X	X
EVERETT COMMUNITY COLLEGE—WA	X	X	X		X	X		X	X	
FAYETTEVILLE TECHNICAL COMMUNITY COLLEGE—NC	X	X	X	X	X	X	X	X		
FINGER LAKES COMMUNITY COLLEGE—NY	X	X	X		X	X	X	X		
FLORIDA KEYS COMMUNITY COLLEGE—FL	X	X	X	X		X		X		
FOX VALLEY TECHNICAL COLLEGE—WI	X		X	X		X			X	
FULTON-MONTGOMERY COMMUNITY COLLEGE—NY	X	X	X	X	X	X	X	X	X	X

INSTITUTION	ANY PRIOR LEARNING ASSESSMENT	ADVANCED PLACEMENT	CLEP	ACT/PEP	DANTES	CHALLENGE EXAM	ACE/PONSI	ACE/MILITARY	INDIVIDUAL ASSESSMENT	ASSESSMENT OF CERTIFICATES
GARLAND COUNTY COMMUNITY COLLEGE—AR	X	X	X			X	X	X	X	
GARRETT COMMUNITY COLLEGE—MD	X	X	X	X	X	X		X	X	X
GASTON COLLEGE—NC	X	X	X			X		X		
GENESEE COMMUNITY COLLEGE—NY	X	X	X		X	X		X	X	X
GERMANNA COMMUNITY COLLEGE—VA	X	X	X			X	X	X		
GLEN OAKS COMMUNITY COLLEGE—MI	X	X	X			X		X		
GLENDALE COMMUNITY COLLEGE—AZ	X	X	X	X	X	X	X	X	X	X
GRAND RAPIDS COMMUNITY COLLEGE—MI	X	X	X	X		X		X	X	X
GREAT LAKES JUNIOR COLLEGE OF BUSINESS—MI	X							X		X
GREEN RIVER COMMUNITY COLLEGE—WA	X	X	X		X	X	X	X	X	
GREENVILLE TECHNICAL COLLEGE—SC	X	X	X		X	X		X		
GUILFORD TECHNICAL COMMUNITY COLLEGE—NC	X	X	X		X	X		X	X	X
HARFORD COMMUNITY COLLEGE—MD	X	X	X		X	X	X	X		
HARRISBURG AREA COMMUNITY COLLEGE-HARRISBURG—PA	X	X	X	X		X		X	X	X
HAYWOOD COMMUNITY COLLEGE—NC	X							X		
HESSTON COLLEGE—KS	X		X			X		X		X
HIGHLINE COMMUNITY COLLEGE—WA	X	X				X		X		
HOCKING TECHNICAL COLLEGE—OH	X	X	X	X	X	X	X	X	X	X

INSTITUTION	ANY PRIOR LEARNING ASSESSMENT	ADVANCED PLACEMENT	CLEP	ACT/PEP	DANTES	CHALLENGE EXAM	ACE/ PONSI	ACE/MILITARY	INDIVIDUAL ASSESSMENT	ASSESSMENT OF CERTIFICATES
HOLY CROSS COLLEGE—IN	X	X	X							
HOLYOKE COMMUNITY COLLEGE—MA	X	X	X	X	X	X	X	X		X
HORRY-GEORGETOWN TECHNICAL COLLEGE—SC	X	X	X		X	X	X	X	X	
HOUSTON COMMUNITY COLLEGE SYSTEM—TX	X	X	X		X	X		X	X	X
HOWARD COUNTY JUNIOR COLLEGE DISTRICT—TX	X	X	X			X		X		
HUDSON VALLEY COMMUNITY COLLEGE—NY	X	X	X	X	X	X	X	X	X	
INDEPENDENCE COMMUNITY COLLEGE—KS	X	X				X		X		
INDIAN HILLS COMMUNITY COLLEGE—IA	X	X	X		X	X				
INTERBORO INSTITUTE—NY	X	X	X	X		X				
IOWA LAKES COMMUNITY COLLEGE—IA	X	X	X	X	X	X	X	X	X	X
IVY TECH STATE COLLEGE-CENTRAL INDIANA—IN	X	X	X	X	X	X		X	X	X
IVY TECH STATE COLLEGE-LAFAYETTE—IN	X	X	X	X	X	X		X	X	
IVY TECH STATE COLLEGE-SOUTHWEST—IN	X	X						X	X	
J. SARGEANT REYNOLDS COMMUNITY COLLEGE—VA	X	X	X		X	X	X	X		
JAMES SPRUNT COMMUNITY COLLEGE—NC	X	X	X	X	X	X	X	X	X	
JEFFERSON COMMUNITY COLLEGE—NY	X		X	X	X	X	X	X		
JEFFERSON DAVIS COMMUNITY COLLEGE-BREWTON CAMPUS—AL	X	X				X		X		
JEFFERSON STATE COMMUNITY COLLEGE—AL	X	X	X					X		

INSTITUTION	ANY PRIOR LEARNING ASSESSMENT	ADVANCED PLACEMENT	CLEP	ACT/PEP	DANTES	CHALLENGE EXAM	ACE/ PONSI	ACE/MILITARY	INDIVIDUAL ASSESSMENT	ASSESSMENT OF CERTIFICATES
JOHN C. CALHOUN STATE COMMUNITY COLLEGE—AL	X	X	X	X	X	X	X	X	X	X
JOHN WOOD COMMUNITY COLLEGE—IL	X	X	X	X	X	X	X	X	X	X
JOLIET JUNIOR COLLEGE—IL	X		X		X	X		X		
KANKAKEE COMMUNITY COLLEGE—IL	X	X	X	X	X	X		X		
KELLOGG COMMUNITY COLLEGE—MI	X	X	X	X	X	X	X	X	X	X
KENT STATE UNIVERSITY-STARK CAMPUS—OH	X	X	X							
KENT STATE UNIVERSITY-TRUMBULL REGIONAL CAMPUS—OH	X	X	X		X	X		X	X	X
KEYSTONE COLLEGE—PA	X		X			X		X		X
KIRTLAND COMMUNITY COLLEGE—MI	X	X	X		X			X		
KISHWAUKEE COLLEGE—IL	X	X	X		X	X		X	X	
LACKAWANNA JUNIOR COLLEGE—PA	X	X	X		X	X	X	X	X	X
LAKE MICHIGAN COLLEGE—MI	X	X	X		X	X	X	X	X	
LAKEWOOD COMMUNITY COLLEGE—MN	X	X	X		X	X		X	X	X
LANE COMMUNITY COLLEGE—OR	X	X	X		X	X	X	X	X	X
LANSING COMMUNITY COLLEGE—MI	X	X	X		X	X		X	X	X
LAREDO COMMUNITY COLLEGE—TX	X	X	X			X				
LEEWARD COMMUNITY COLLEGE—HI	X	X	X		X	X		X	X	
LINN-BENTON COMMUNITY COLLEGE—OR										

INSTITUTION	ANY PRIOR LEARNING ASSESSMENT	ADVANCED PLACEMENT	CLEP	ACT/PEP	DANTES	CHALLENGE EXAM	ACE/ PONSI	ACE/MILITARY	INDIVIDUAL ASSESSMENT	ASSESSMENT OF CERTIFICATES
LOUISIANA STATE UNIVERSITY- ALEXANDRIA—LA	X	X	X			X	X	X		
LOUISIANA STATE UNIVERSITY- EUNICE—LA	X	X	X	X		X		X		X
LURLEEN B. WALLACE STATE JUNIOR COLLEGE—AL	X	X	X			X		X		
MACCORMAC COLLEGE—IL										
MADISONVILLE COMMUNITY COLLEGE—KY	X	X	X	X		X	X	X		X
MANCHESTER COMMUNITY TECHNICAL COLLEGE—CT	X		X		X	X		X		
MARIAN COURT COLLEGE—MA	X					X			X	
MARION MILITARY INSTITUTE—AL										
MASSASOIT COMMUNITY COLLEGE—MA	X	X	X	X	X	X	X	X	X	X
MAYSVILLE COMMUNITY COLLEGE—KY	X	X	X	X	X	X	X	X	X	
MENDOCINO COLLEGE—CA	X	X				X	X	X		
MERCER COUNTY COMMUNITY COLLEGE—NJ	X	X	X	X	X	X		X	X	X
MESA COMMUNITY COLLEGE—AZ	X	X	X	X	X	X	X	X	X	X
MIAMI UNIVERSITY- MIDDLETOWN—OH	X	X	X			X		X		
MID-STATE TECHNICAL COLLEGE-MAIN CAMPUS—WI										
MIDDLESEX COUNTY COLLEGE—NJ	X	X	X	X	X			X		
MIDLAND COLLEGE—TX	X	X	X			X		X	X	X
MISSISSIPPI COUNTY COMMUNITY COLLEGE—AR	X	X	X		X	X		X	X	X
MOHAVE COMMUNITY COLLEGE—AZ	X		X		X	X		X		

INSTITUTION	ANY PRIOR LEARNING ASSESSMENT	ADVANCED PLACEMENT	CLEP	ACT/PEP	DANTES	CHALLENGE EXAM	ACE/ PONSI	ACE/MILITARY	INDIVIDUAL ASSESSMENT	ASSESSMENT OF CERTIFICATES
MONROE COUNTY COMMUNITY COLLEGE—MI										
MONTCALM COMMUNITY COLLEGE—MI	X		X		X	X		X		
MORAINE VALLEY COMMUNITY COLLEGE—IL	X	X	X	X	X	X			X	X
MORGAN COMMUNITY COLLEGE—CO	X	X	X	X	X	X	X	X	X	
MOUNT ALOYSIUS COLLEGE—PA	X	X	X	X		X			X	
MOUNTAIN VIEW COLLEGE—TX	X		X		X	X		X	X	X
MT. HOOD COMMUNITY COLLEGE—OR	X	X	X			X		X	X	
MURRAY STATE COLLEGE—OK	X		X			X	X	X	X	
NASH COMMUNITY COLLEGE—NC	X		X					X		
NASSAU COMMUNITY COLLEGE—NY	X	X	X		X	X	X		X	X
NAUGATUCK VALLEY COMMUNITY-TECHNICAL COLLEGE—CT	X	X	X			X			X	X
NEOSHO COUNTY COMMUNITY COLLEGE—KS	X		X	X	X	X		X		
NEW ENGLAND INSTITUTE OF TECHNOLOGY—RI	X		X		X	X	X	X	X	X
NEW HAMPSHIRE TECHNICAL COLLEGE AT MANCHESTER—NH	X	X	X	X		X		X	X	
NEW MEXICO JUNIOR COLLEGE—NM	X	X	X		X	X		X		
NEW MEXICO MILITARY INSTITUTE—NM	X	X	X		X	X	X	X		
NORMANDALE COMMUNITY COLLEGE—MN	X	X	X		X	X		X	X	
NORTH CENTRAL MISSOURI COLLEGE—MO	X		X		X	X	X	X		

INSTITUTION	ANY PRIOR LEARNING ASSESSMENT	ADVANCED PLACEMENT	CLEP	ACT/PEP	DANTES	CHALLENGE EXAM	ACE/ PONSI	ACE/MILITARY	INDIVIDUAL ASSESSMENT	ASSESSMENT OF CERTIFICATES
NORTH CENTRAL TECHNICAL COLLEGE—OH	X		X	X		X		X	X	X
NORTH CENTRAL TEXAS COLLEGE—TX	X	X	X	X	X	X		X	X	
NORTH HARRIS MONTGOMERY COMMUNITY COLLEGE DISTRICT—TX	X	X	X	X		X		X	X	X
NORTH SHORE COMMUNITY COLLEGE—MA	X		X	X	X				X	X
NORTHAMPTON COUNTY AREA COMMUNITY COLLEGE—PA	X	X	X	X	X	X	X	X		
NORTHEAST COMMUNITY COLLEGE—NE	X	X	X		X		X	X		
NORTHERN MAINE TECHNICAL COLLEGE—ME	X	X	X	X	X	X		X	X	
NORTHLAND COMMUNITY AND TECHNICAL COLLEGE—MN	X	X	X		X			X		
NORTHWEST ARKANSAS COMMUNITY COLLEGE—AR	X	X	X			X				
NORTHWESTERN COLLEGE—OH	X	X							X	
NORTHWESTERN MICHIGAN COLLEGE—MI	X	X	X	X				X	X	
OHIO UNIVERSITY EASTERN CAMPUS—OH										
OWENS COMMUNITY COLLEGE—OH	X	X	X		X	X		X	X	X
OWENSBORO COMMUNITY COLLEGE—KY	X	X	X	X	X	X	X	X		
OZARKA TECHNICAL COLLEGE—AR	X	X	X		X	X		X	X	
PAUL SMITH'S COLLEGE OF ARTS AND SCIENCE—NY	X	X	X	X	X	X		X	X	
PEIRCE COLLEGE—PA	X	X	X		X	X		X		
PENNSYLVANIA INSTITUTE OF TECHNOLOGY—PA	X		X		X	X		X	X	X

INSTITUTION	ANY PRIOR LEARNING ASSESSMENT	ADVANCED PLACEMENT	CLEP	ACT/PEP	DANTES	CHALLENGE EXAM	ACE/PONSI	ACE/MILITARY	INDIVIDUAL ASSESSMENT	ASSESSMENT OF CERTIFICATES
PENSACOLA JUNIOR COLLEGE—FL	X	X	X			X		X	X	
PITT COMMUNITY COLLEGE—NC	X		X			X		X		
PRESENTATION COLLEGE—SD	X		X	X		X			X	
PRESTONSBURG COMMUNITY COLLEGE—KY	X	X	X	X	X	X	X	X	X	
QUINSIGAMOND COMMUNITY COLLEGE—MA	X	X	X	X	X	X	X	X	X	X
RARITAN VALLEY COMMUNITY COLLEGE—NJ	X	X	X		X	X	X	X	X	X
READING AREA COMMUNITY COLLEGE—PA	X	X	X	X		X			X	
REINHARDT COLLEGE—GA	X	X	X							
RENTON TECHNICAL COLLEGE—WA	X	X	X						X	
RICHMOND COMMUNITY COLLEGE—NC	X	X	X			X		X		
RICKS COLLEGE—ID	X	X	X			X				
RIO SALADO COMMUNITY COLLEGE—AZ	X	X	X	X	X		X	X		X
ROANOKE-CHOWAN COMMUNITY COLLEGE—NC	X	X	X		X	X		X		
ROBESON COMMUNITY COLLEGE—NC	X	X	X		X	X		X		
SAINT CLOUD TECHNICAL COLLEGE—MN	X	X	X		X	X		X	X	
SALEM COMMUNITY COLLEGE—NJ	X		X		X	X	X	X	X	
SAN JOSE CITY COLLEGE—CA	X		X		X	X		X		
SANDHILLS COMMUNITY COLLEGE—NC	X	X	X		X	X			X	X
SANTA FE COMMUNITY COLLEGE—NM	X	X	X		X	X		X		

INSTITUTION	ANY PRIOR LEARNING ASSESSMENT	ADVANCED PLACEMENT	CLEP	ACT/PEP	DANTES	CHALLENGE EXAM	ACE/PONSI	ACE/MILITARY	INDIVIDUAL ASSESSMENT	ASSESSMENT OF CERTIFICATES
SCHENECTADY COUNTY COMMUNITY COLLEGE—NY	X	X	X			X		X	X	
SCHOOLCRAFT COLLEGE—MI	X	X	X		X	X		X		
SHORTER COLLEGE—AR										X
SINCLAIR COMMUNITY COLLEGE—OH	X	X	X		X	X	X	X	X	
SNOW COLLEGE—UT	X	X	X		X	X	X	X		
SOUTHERN STATE COMMUNITY COLLEGE—OH	X	X	X	X	X	X	X	X	X	
SOUTHWEST MISSISSIPPI COMMUNITY COLLEGE—MS	X	X	X					X		
SOUTHWESTERN OREGON COMMUNITY COLLEGE—OR	X		X			X		X	X	
SPARTANBURG METHODIST COLLEGE—SC	X	X	X							
SPOKANE FALLS COMMUNITY COLLEGE—WA	X	X			X	X		X		
SPRINGFIELD TECHNICAL COMMUNITY COLLEGE—MA	X	X	X		X	X		X	X	
ST. CHARLES COUNTY COMMUNITY COLLEGE—MO	X	X	X	X	X	X	X	X		
ST. CLAIR COUNTY COMMUNITY COLLEGE—MI	X	X	X			X			X	
ST. JOSEPH'S HOSPITAL HEALTH CENTER SCHOOL OF NURSING—NY	X	X	X		X	X				
STANLY COMMUNITY COLLEGE—NC										
STATE TECHNICAL INSTITUTE AT MEMPHIS—TN	X	X	X		X	X		X	X	X
SUFFOLK COUNTY COMMUNITY COLLEGE- AMMERMAN CAMPUS—NY	X	X	X		X	X			X	
SUNY COLLEGE OF AGRIC AND TECHN AT COBLESKILL—NY	X	X	X			X	X	X		

INSTITUTION	ANY PRIOR LEARNING ASSESSMENT	ADVANCED PLACEMENT	CLEP	ACT/PEP	DANTES	CHALLENGE EXAM	ACE/ PONSI	ACE/MILITARY	INDIVIDUAL ASSESSMENT	ASSESSMENT OF CERTIFICATES
SUNY COLLEGE OF TECHNOLOGY AT ALFRED—NY	X	X	X			X		X		X
SUNY ULSTER COUNTY COMMUNITY COLLEGE—NY	X	X	X	X	X	X	X	X	X	
SURRY COMMUNITY COLLEGE—NC	X		X		X	X		X		
TACOMA COMMUNITY COLLEGE—WA	X	X	X			X		X		
THE COLLEGE OF WEST VIRGINIA—WV	X	X	X	X	X	X	X	X	X	X
THOMAS NELSON COMMUNITY COLLEGE—VA	X	X	X		X	X		X	X	
THREE RIVERS COMMUNITY COLLEGE—MO	X	X	X					X		
THREE RIVERS COMMUNITY-TECHNICAL COLLEGE—CT	X	X	X		X	X	X	X	X	X
TRI-COUNTY TECHNICAL COLLEGE—SC	X	X	X	X	X	X		X	X	X
TRINITY VALLEY COMMUNITY COLLEGE—TX	X	X	X	X				X		
TROCAIRE COLLEGE—NY	X	X	X	X	X	X	X	X	X	X
TRUETT-MCCONNELL COLLEGE—GA	X	X	X							
TYLER JUNIOR COLLEGE—TX	X	X	X		X	X		X	X	
UMPQUA COMMUNITY COLLEGE—OR	X	X	X	X	X	X	X	X		X
UNION COUNTY COLLEGE—NJ	X		X		X	X				
UTAH VALLEY STATE COLLEGE—UT	X	X	X	X	X	X		X	X	X
VALLEY FORGE MILITARY COLLEGE—PA	X	X	X		X		X	X		
VERMONT TECHNICAL COLLEGE—VT	X	X	X		X	X		X	X	
VERNON REGIONAL JUNIOR COLLEGE—TX	X	X	X	X	X	X	X	X		

INSTITUTION	ANY PRIOR LEARNING ASSESSMENT	ADVANCED PLACEMENT	CLEP	ACT/PEP	DANTES	CHALLENGE EXAM	ACE/ PONSI	ACE/MILITARY	INDIVIDUAL ASSESSMENT	ASSESSMENT OF CERTIFICATES
VICTORIA COLLEGE—TX	X	X	X	X		X				
VILLA MARIA COLLEGE BUFFALO—NY	X	X	X	X	X	X		X	X	
VINCENNES UNIVERSITY—IN	X	X	X	X	X	X	X	X	X	X
WAKE TECHNICAL COMMUNITY COLLEGE—NC	X		X		X	X			X	X
WASHINGTON STATE COMMUNITY COLLEGE—OH	X	X	X			X		X	X	
WAUKESHA COUNTY TECHNICAL COLLEGE—WI	X		X			X		X	X	X
WENATCHEE VALLEY COLLEGE—WA	X		X			X		X		
WEST HILLS COMMUNITY COLLEGE—CA	X	X	X		X	X		X		
WEST VIRGINIA UNIVERSITY AT PARKERSBURG—WV	X	X	X			X		X		X
WESTERN NEBRASKA COMMUNITY COLLEGE—NE	X	X	X			X		X	X	
WESTERN OKLAHOMA STATE COLLEGE—OK	X		X	X	X	X	X	X	X	X
WESTERN PIEDMONT COMMUNITY COLLEGE—NC	X	X	X		X	X				
WESTERN TEXAS COLLEGE—TX	X	X	X	X	X			X		
WHATCOM COMMUNITY COLLEGE—WA	X	X	X	X	X	X	X	X	X	
WILSON TECHNICAL COMMUNITY COLLEGE—NC	X		X			X		X		X
YAVAPAI COLLEGE—AZ	X	X	X		X	X				X
YORK COLLEGE—NE	X	X	X		X	X		X	X	X
YUBA COLLEGE—CA	X	X	X	X	X	X		X		
ALBERTUS MAGNUS COLLEGE—CT	X		X	X	X	X	X	X	X	

INSTITUTION	ANY PRIOR LEARNING ASSESSMENT	ADVANCED PLACEMENT	CLEP	ACT/PEP	DANTES	CHALLENGE EXAM	ACE/ PONSI	ACE/MILITARY	INDIVIDUAL ASSESSMENT	ASSESSMENT OF CERTIFICATES
SPECIALIZED INSTITUTIONS (Theological seminaries, Bible colleges, and other institutions offering degrees in religion)										
AQUINAS INSTITUTE OF THEOLOGY—MO										
ARLINGTON BAPTIST COLLEGE—TX										
ASBURY THEOLOGICAL SEMINARY—KY										
BAPTIST BIBLE COLLEGE AND SEMINARY—PA	X		X		X	X	X	X	X	
BARCLAY COLLEGE—KS	X	X	X	X	X			X	X	
BIBLICAL THEOLOGICAL SEMINARY—PA										
CENTRAL BAPTIST THEOLOGICAL SEMINARY—KS										
CHICAGO THEOLOGICAL SEMINARY—IL										
CHRIST THE KING SEMINARY—NY										
CHURCH DIVINITY SCHOOL OF THE PACIFIC—CA										
CHURCH OF GOD SCHOOL OF THEOLOGY—IN										
CLEVELAND COLLEGE OF JEWISH STUDIES—OH										
COLUMBIA INTERNATIONAL UNIVERSITY—SC	X	X	X		X			X		
COLUMBIA THEOLOGICAL SEMINARY—GA										
CONCORDIA THEOLOGICAL SEMINARY—IN										
COVENANT THEOLOGICAL SEMINARY—MO	X					X				
DALLAS THEOLOGICAL SEMINARY—TX	X					X				

INSTITUTION	ANY PRIOR LEARNING ASSESSMENT	ADVANCED PLACEMENT	CLEP	ACT/PEP	DANTES	CHALLENGE EXAM	ACE/ PONSI	ACE/MILITARY	INDIVIDUAL ASSESSMENT	ASSESSMENT OF CERTIFICATES
DENVER CONSERVATIVE BAPTIST SEMINARY—CO	X								X	
EDEN THEOLOGICAL SEMINARY—MO										
EPISCOPAL THEOLOGICAL SEMINARY OF THE SOUTHWEST—TX										
EUGENE BIBLE COLLEGE—OR	X		X					X	X	
FAITH BAPTIST BIBLE COLLEGE AND SEMINARY—IA	X	X	X			X		X	X	
FLORIDA BAPTIST THEOLOGICAL COLLEGE—FL	X	X	X		X		X	X		
GARRETT-EVANGELICAL THEOLOGICAL SEMINARY—IL										
GOD'S BIBLE SCHOOL AND COLLEGE—OH	X		X							
GOLDEN GATE BAPTIST SEMINARY—CA										
GORDON-CONWELL THEOLOGICAL SEMINARY—MA										
HARTFORD SEMINARY—CT	X								X	X
HEBREW UNION COLLEGE CALIFORNIA BRANCH—CA	X								X	
HEBREW UNION COLLEGE-JEWISH INSTITUTE OF RELIGION—OH										
HELLENIC COLLEGE-HOLY CROSS GRK ORTH SCH OF THEOLOGY—MA	X		X			X			X	
INTERNATIONAL BIBLE COLLEGE—AL	X		X		X		X			
JOHN WESLEY COLLEGE—NC	X		X		X	X	X	X	X	X
KENRICK GLENNON SEMINARY—MO										

INSTITUTION	ANY PRIOR LEARNING ASSESSMENT	ADVANCED PLACEMENT	CLEP	ACT/PEP	DANTES	CHALLENGE EXAM	ACE/PONSI	ACE/MILITARY	INDIVIDUAL ASSESSMENT	ASSESSMENT OF CERTIFICATES
LANCASTER BIBLE COLLEGE—PA	X	X	X		X		X	X	X	X
LEXINGTON THEOLOGICAL SEMINARY—KY										
LOUISVILLE PRESBYTERIAN THEOLOGICAL SEMINARY—KY										
LUTHER SEMINARY—MN										
LUTHERAN BIBLE INSTITUTE OF SEATTLE—WA	X	X	X	X	X		X	X	X	
LUTHERAN SCHOOL OF THEOLOGY AT CHICAGO—IL	X					X				
LUTHERAN THEOLOGICAL SEMINARY AT GETTYSBURG—PA	X					X				
LUTHERAN THEOLOGICAL SEMINARY AT PHILADELPHIA—PA										
MANHATTAN CHRISTIAN COLLEGE—KS	X		X		X	X	X	X	X	X
MARANATHA BAPTIST BIBLE COLLEGE INC—WI	X		X		X			X		
MCCORMICK THEOLOGICAL SEMINARY—IL	X								X	
MEMPHIS THEOLOGICAL SEMINARY—TN										
MENNONITE BRETHREN BIBLICAL SEMINARY—CA	X					X				
METHODIST THEOLOGICAL SCHOOL OHIO—OH										
MICHIGAN CHRISTIAN COLLEGE—MI	X	X	X		X	X	X	X	X	
MID AMERICA BAPTIST SEMINARY—TN										
MIDWESTERN BAPTIST THEOLOGICAL SEMINARY—MO										
MINNESOTA BIBLE COLLEGE—MN	X	X	X					X		

INSTITUTION	ANY PRIOR LEARNING ASSESSMENT	ADVANCED PLACEMENT	CLEP	ACT/PEP	DANTES	CHALLENGE EXAM	ACE/ PONSI	ACE/MILITARY	INDIVIDUAL ASSESSMENT	ASSESSMENT OF CERTIFICATES
NASHOTAH HOUSE—WI										
NAZARENE BIBLE COLLEGE—CO	X		X			X		X		
NORTH CENTRAL BIBLE COLLEGE—MN	X	X	X		X	X		X	X	
NORTHERN BAPTIST THEOLOGICAL SEMINARY—IL										
NORTHWEST COLLEGE OF THE ASSEMBLIES OF GOD—WA	X	X	X		X	X	X	X	X	
NOTRE DAME SEMINARY GRADUATE SCHOOL OF THEOLOGY—LA										
OBLATE SCHOOL OF THEOLOGY—TX	X					X	X			
PHILADELPHIA COLLEGE OF BIBLE—PA	X	X	X					X	X	
PIEDMONT BIBLE COLLEGE—NC	X		X							
PITTSBURGH THEOLOGICAL SEMINARY—PA										
PONTIFICAL COLLEGE JOSEPHINUM—OH										
PUGET SOUND CHRISTIAN COLLEGE—WA	X	X	X	X	X	X	X	X	X	
REFORMED BIBLE COLLEGE—MI	X	X	X		X	X		X	X	
ROANOKE BIBLE COLLEGE—NC	X	X	X	X	X			X		
SACRED HEART SCHOOL OF THEOLOGY—WI	X								X	
SAINT JOHN'S SEMINARY—MA	X					X				
SAINT JOHN'S SEMINARY COLLEGE—CA	X	X								
SAINT JOSEPH'S SEMINARY AND COLLEGE—NY										

INSTITUTION	ANY PRIOR LEARNING ASSESSMENT	ADVANCED PLACEMENT	CLEP	ACT/PEP	DANTES	CHALLENGE EXAM	ACE/ PONSI	ACE/MILITARY	INDIVIDUAL ASSESSMENT	ASSESSMENT OF CERTIFICATES
SAINT PATRICK'S SEMINARY—CA										
SAN FRANCISCO THEOLOGICAL SEMINARY—CA										
SCHOOL OF THEOLOGY AT CLAREMONT—CA										
SEABURY-WESTERN THEOLOGICAL SEMINARY—IL										
SEMINARY OF THE IMMACULATE CONCEPTION—NY										
SOUTHERN BAPTIST THEOLOGICAL SEMINARY—KY	X		X			X				
SOUTHERN CHRISTIAN UNIVERSITY—AL	X				X		X	X		
TRINITY BIBLE COLLEGE—ND	X	X	X		X	X		X	X	
TRINITY EVANGELICAL DIVINITY SCHOOL—IL	X		X			X		X		X
TRINITY LUTHERAN SEMINARY—OH										
UNION THEOLOGICAL SEMINARY IN VIRGINIA—VA	X					X	X		X	
UNITED THEOLOGICAL SEMINARY—OH										
UNIVERSITY OF SAINT MARY OF THE LAKE—IL										
WARTBURG THEOLOGICAL SEMINARY—IA										
WESTERN CONSERVATIVE BAPTIST SEMINARY—OR	X					X				
WESTMINSTER THEOLOGICAL SEMINARY—PA										
WINEBRENNER THEOLOGICAL SEMINARY—OH										

INSTITUTION	ANY PRIOR LEARNING ASSESSMENT	ADVANCED PLACEMENT	CLEP	ACT/PEP	DANTES	CHALLENGE EXAM	ACE/ PONSI	ACE/MILITARY	INDIVIDUAL ASSESSMENT	ASSESSMENT OF CERTIFICATES
SPECIALIZED INSTITUTIONS (Medical schools and medical centers)										
BAYLOR COLLEGE OF MEDICINE—TX										
KIRKSVILLE COLLEGE OF OSTEOPATHIC MEDICINE—MO										
MEDICAL COLLEGE OF GEORGIA—GA	X		X	X		X			X	X
MEHARRY MEDICAL COLLEGE—TN	X	X	X	X	X	X		X		
MOUNT SINAI SCHOOL OF MEDICINE—NY										
NEW YORK MEDICAL COLLEGE—NY	X								X	
PONCE SCHOOL OF MEDICINE—PR										
RUSH UNIVERSITY—IL	X			X		X				
SUNY HEALTH SCIENCE CENTER AT SYRACUSE—NY	X	X	X	X		X		X		
THE UNIVERSITY OF TEXAS MEDICAL BRANCH-GALVESTON—TX										
UNIVERSITY OF NEBRASKA MEDICAL CENTER—NE	X	X	X		X	X		X		
UNIVERSITY OF TENNESSEE-MEMPHIS—TN										
OTHER SEPARATE HEALTH PROFESSION SCHOOLS										
BELLIN COLLEGE OF NURSING—WI	X	X	X	X		X			X	X
CLARKSON COLLEGE—NE	X	X	X				X	X		
CLEVELAND CHIROPRACTIC COLLEGE OF LOS ANGELES—CA										

INSTITUTION	ANY PRIOR LEARNING ASSESSMENT	ADVANCED PLACEMENT	CLEP	ACT/PEP	DANTES	CHALLENGE EXAM	ACE/ PONSI	ACE/MILITARY	INDIVIDUAL ASSESSMENT	ASSESSMENT OF CERTIFICATES
DEACONESS COLLEGE OF NURSING—MO	X	X	X		X	X		X		
DR. WILLIAM SCHOLL COLLEGE OF PODIATRIC—IL										
ILLINOIS COLLEGE OF OPTOMETRY—IL										
LOGAN COLLEGE OF CHIROPRACTIC—MO	X	X	X	X	X			X		
LUTHERAN COLLEGE OF HEALTH PROFESSIONS—IN	X		X							
MEDCENTER ONE COLLEGE OF NURSING—ND	X	X				X			X	
MENNONITE COLLEGE OF NURSING—IL	X	X				X				
MOUNT CARMEL COLLEGE OF NURSING—OH										
NEW ENGLAND COLLEGE OF OPTOMETRY—MA										
OHIO COLLEGE OF PODIATRIC MEDICINE—OH	X								X	
PALMER COLLEGE OF CHIROPRACTIC—IA										
PENNSYLVANIA COLLEGE OF PODIATRIC MEDICINE—PA	X					X				
SAINT JOSEPH COLLEGE OF NURSING—IL	X			X		X			X	
SAINT LUKE'S COLLEGE—KS										
WESTERN STATES CHIROPRACTIC COLLEGE—OR										
SCHOOLS OF ENGINEERING AND TECHNOLOGY										
CAPITOL COLLEGE—MD	X	X	X	X	X	X	X	X		
DEVRY INSTITUTE OF TECHNOLOGY—IL	X		X		X	X		X		
GMI ENGINEERING AND MANAGEMENT INSTITUTE—MI	X	X				X				

INSTITUTION	ANY PRIOR LEARNING ASSESSMENT	ADVANCED PLACEMENT	CLEP	ACT/PEP	DANTES	CHALLENGE EXAM	ACE/PONSI	ACE/MILITARY	INDIVIDUAL ASSESSMENT	ASSESSMENT OF CERTIFICATES
HENRY COGSWELL COLLEGE—WA	X		X	X		X	X	X	X	
OREGON INSTITUTE OF TECHNOLOGY—OR	X	X	X		X	X		X	X	
PARKS COLLEGE OF SAINT LOUIS UNIVERSITY—IL	X	X	X	X		X				X
SOUTH DAKOTA SCHOOL OF MINES AND TECHNOLOGY—SD	X	X	X			X		X		
WENTWORTH INSTITUTE OF TECHNOLOGY—MA	X	X	X			X		X	X	X
SCHOOLS OF BUSINESS AND MANAGEMENT										
AMERICAN GRADUATE SCHOOL OF INTERNATIONAL MGMT—AZ	X		X		X					
BENTLEY COLLEGE—MA	X	X	X	X	X	X	X	X	X	
COLUMBIA COLLEGE—PR	X					X		X	X	
DAVENPORT COLLEGE—MI	X		X		X	X	X	X	X	X
DETROIT COLLEGE OF BUSINESS-DEARBORN—MI	X	X	X	X	X	X	X	X	X	X
FRANKLIN UNIVERSITY—OH	X	X	X	X	X	X	X	X	X	
INDIANA INSTITUTE OF TECHNOLOGY—IN	X		X		X		X	X	X	
LAKE FOREST GRADUATE SCHOOL OF MANAGEMENT—IL										
LYNN UNIVERSITY—FL	X	X	X	X	X	X	X	X	X	X
MENLO COLLEGE—CA	X	X	X	X	X	X	X	X	X	
NATIONAL COLLEGE—SD	X		X	X	X	X	X	X	X	X
NICHOLS COLLEGE—MA	X	X	X	X	X	X	X	X	X	

INSTITUTION	ANY PRIOR LEARNING ASSESSMENT	ADVANCED PLACEMENT	CLEP	ACT/PEP	DANTES	CHALLENGE EXAM	ACE/ PONSI	ACE/MILITARY	INDIVIDUAL ASSESSMENT	ASSESSMENT OF CERTIFICATES
ROBERT MORRIS COLLEGE—IL	X	X	X					X		
ROBERT MORRIS COLLEGE—PA	X		X	X	X	X		X		
THE HARTFORD GRADUATE CENTER—CT										
THOMAS COLLEGE—ME	X	X	X		X	X	X	X	X	
TIFFIN UNIVERSITY—OH	X	X	X	X	X	X	X	X	X	
UNIVERSITY OF PHOENIX-PHOENIX CAMPUS—AZ	X	X	X	X	X		X	X	X	X
WALSH COLLEGE OF ACCOUNTANCY AND BUSINESS ADMIN—MI										
WEBBER COLLEGE—FL	X	X	X		X			X		
SCHOOLS OF ART, MUSIC, AND DESIGN										
AMERICAN CONSERVATORY THEATER—PA										
ART INSTITUTE OF SOUTHERN CALIFORNIA—CA	X					X		X		
CALIFORNIA INSTITUTE OF THE ARTS—CA	X	X								
CENTER FOR CREATIVE STUDIES COLLEGE OF ART & DESIGN—MI	X		X					X		
CORNISH COLLEGE OF THE ARTS—WA										
HARRINGTON INSTITUTE OF INTERIOR DESIGN—IL	X		X							
OTIS COLLEGE OF ART AND DESIGN—CA										
PACIFIC NORTHWEST COLLEGE OF ART—OR	X	X								
PRATT INSTITUTE-MAIN—NY										

INSTITUTION	ANY PRIOR LEARNING ASSESSMENT	ADVANCED PLACEMENT	CLEP	ACT/PEP	DANTES	CHALLENGE EXAM	ACE/ PONSI	ACE/MILITARY	INDIVIDUAL ASSESSMENT	ASSESSMENT OF CERTIFICATES
RINGLING SCHOOL OF ART AND DESIGN—FL	X								X	
THE BOSTON CONSERVATORY—MA	X	X	X	X	X		X	X	X	
THE JUILLIARD SCHOOL—NY										
SCHOOLS OF LAW										
ALBANY LAW SCHOOL—NY										
SOUTH TEXAS COLLEGE OF LAW—TX										
SOUTHWESTERN UNIVERSITY SCHOOL OF LAW—CA										
THE UNIVERSITY OF WEST LOS ANGELES—CA	X		X		X	X	X	X		
THOMAS M. COOLEY LAW SCHOOL—MI										
UNIVERSITY OF CALIFORNIA HASTINGS COLLEGE OF LAW—CA										
WILLIAM MITCHELL COLLEGE OF LAW—MN										
TEACHERS COLLEGES										
CAMBRIDGE COLLEGE—MA	X		X	X	X	X	X	X	X	
HARRIS-STOWE STATE COLLEGE—MO										
MARTIN LUTHER COLLEGE—MN	X	X								
OTHER SPECIALIZED INSTITUTIONS										
ALFRED ADLER INSTITUTE OF MINNESOTA—MN										
CALIFORNIA INSTITUTE OF INTEGRAL STUDIES—CA	X	X	X		X		X	X	X	

INSTITUTION	ANY PRIOR LEARNING ASSESSMENT	ADVANCED PLACEMENT	CLEP	ACT/PEP	DANTES	CHALLENGE EXAM	ACE/ PONSI	ACE/MILITARY	INDIVIDUAL ASSESSMENT	ASSESSMENT OF CERTIFICATES
CENTER FOR HUMANISTIC STUDIES—MI										
MAINE MARITIME ACADEMY—ME	X	X	X	X	X	X	X	X	X	
MASSACHUSETTS MARITIME ACADEMY—MA	X	X	X		X	X		X		
MASSACHUSETTS SCHOOL OF PROFESSIONAL PSYCHOLOGY—MA										
MONTEREY INSTITUTE OF INTERNATIONAL STUDIES—CA										
NAVAL POSTGRADUATE SCHOOL—CA										
PHILLIPS GRADUATE INSTITUTE—CA										
REGENT UNIVERSITY—VA										
SAYBROOK INSTITUTE—CA										
SCHOOL FOR INTERNATIONAL TRAINING—VT	X	X	X	X	X		X	X		
SUNY MARITIME COLLEGE—NY	X							X		X
THE FIELDING INSTITUTE—CA										
UNITED STATES ARMY COMMAND AND GENERAL STAFF COLLEGE—KS										
UNITED STATES COAST GUARD ACADEMY—CT										
UNITED STATES MERCHANT MARINE ACADEMY—NY	X	X	X			X				
WISCONSIN SCHOOL OF PROFESSIONAL PSYCHOLOGY—WI										

INSTITUTION	ANY PRIOR LEARNING ASSESSMENT	ADVANCED PLACEMENT	CLEP	ACT/PEP	DANTES	CHALLENGE EXAM	ACE/ PONSI	ACE/MILITARY	INDIVIDUAL ASSESSMENT	ASSESSMENT OF CERTIFICATES
TRIBAL COLLEGES										
DULL KNIFE MEMORIAL COLLEGE—MT										
SINTE GLESKA UNIVERSITY—SD	X					X				
STONE CHILD COLLEGE—MT										
CARNEGIE FOUNDATION CLASSIFICATION CODES MISSING										
BOARD OF TRUSTEES-STATE INSTS OF HIGHER LEARNING—PR										
CITY COLLEGES OF CHICAGO-CENTRAL OFFICE—IL	X	X	X	X	X				X	
CROUSE IRVING MEMORIAL HOSPITAL SCHOOL OF NURSIN—NY	X	X	X						X	X
ELAINE P. NUNEZ COMMUNITY COLLEGE—LA	X	X	X		X	X		X	X	X
HERITAGE BIBLE COLLEGE—NC	X							X	X	
INTER AMERICAN UNIV OF PUERTO RICO-CENTRAL OFFICE—PR	X	X	X		X	X		X	X	
INTERNATIONAL COLLEGE—FL	X	X	X	X	X	X	X	X	X	
LOUISE HARKEY SCHOOL OF NURSING-CABARRUS MEM HOSPITAL—NC	X	X	X			X			X	X
MONTGOMERY COLLEGE-CENTRAL OFFICE—MD	X	X	X	X	X	X		X	X	X
NORTHWEST TECHNICAL COLLEGE-DETROIT LAKES—MN	X		X	X	X	X	X	X	X	X

INSTITUTION	ANY PRIOR LEARNING ASSESSMENT	ADVANCED PLACEMENT	CLEP	ACT/PEP	DANTES	CHALLENGE EXAM	ACE/ PONSI	ACE/MILITARY	INDIVIDUAL ASSESSMENT	ASSESSMENT OF CERTIFICATES
PENNSYLVANIA STATE UNIVERSITY-CENTRAL OFFICE—PA	X	X	X		X	X		X	X	
SAINT JOSEPH'S COLLEGE-MAIN CAMPUS—NY	X	X	X		X		X	X	X	
SOUTHWESTERN COLLEGE—NM	X		X							
SUNY-SYSTEM OFFICE—NY	X	X	X	X	X	X	X	X	X	X
UNIVERSITY OF PUERTO RICO-CENTRAL ADMINISTRATION—PR	X		X	X						

About the Council for Adult and Experiential Learning

CAEL's Background

The Council for Adult and Experiential Learning (CAEL) is a national leader in the field of adult learning and is the preeminent not-for-profit organization coordinating educational services for adults. Since its founding in 1974, under the auspices of the Educational Testing Service (ETS) in Princeton, New Jersey, CAEL has been providing individuals and organizations with the tools and strategies they need for creating practical, effective lifelong learning solutions for their education and training needs.

What Is CAEL's Role in Prior Learning Assessment?

CAEL is a pioneer in the field of Prior Learning Assessment (PLA). Over twenty years ago, CAEL took the lead in articulating the philosophical basis for PLA as well as developing a set of policies and procedures for implementing it in an academically sound manner. Today, in response to the unique needs of adult learners, more colleges conduct prior learning assessment and use the CAEL models as their guide to quality assurance.

CAEL can help individuals prepare for PLA by providing information on portfolio development, directing individuals to appropriate educational institutions, and preparing them for a formal meeting with faculty at those institutions through the following products and services:

◆ Publications

◆ Workshops (both on- and off-campus)

◆ Individual Advising

To learn about the availability of PLA workshops in your area, call the CAEL national office at 312-922-5909.

About Human Capital Research Corporation

Human Capital Research Corporation (HCRC) was established in 1992 to provide educational practitioners, policy makers, and other community stakeholders with the critical information needed to support complex decisions, long-term strategic planning, and educational reform. Our mission is to advance ***opportunity, productivity,*** and ***value*** in the community by ensuring that education policy is based on rigorous analysis. Our promise is to provide our clients with clear, comprehensive examinations of their environments.

HCRC has built a national reputation by merging the multi-disciplinary rigors of quantitative and qualitative analysis with in-depth substantive knowledge of the education enterprise. With education as our exclusive specialty, HCRC stands out in the vast field of private education research and consulting groups. Our ability to listen and discern our clients' needs and capacities and to address policy and programmatic solutions in imaginative ways enables HCRC to compete successfully with the nation's larger leading research organizations.

Our multi-disciplinary research methods include primary survey research, extensive secondary research and analysis, economic modeling and simulation analysis, and qualitative methodologies including focus group research and in-depth interviewing. While our research methods are analytic, academic, and technically rigorous, our communication practices are based on the principle that research must be usable to the client, understood by multiple stakeholders, and designed chiefly to help our clients make lasting, positive change.

HCRC has conducted major studies to support policy decisions in over 20 states. Our client base includes middle schools and high schools, public and private two- and four-year colleges and universities, human service and economic development agencies, state and national higher education associations, state coordinating boards, state financial aid commissions, system and sector governing boards, private education policy research organizations, and private corporations.

For more information about HCRC or to inquire about available publications, please call 1-800-353-9715.

About the Authors

Chantell C. Johnson is a research analyst with Human Capital Research Corporation (HCRC) and is responsible for quantitative and qualitative analysis with an emphasis in program evaluation and design. Chantell has served as principle investigator on a census of early intervention programs in Chicago, and in the development of numerous scholarship and faculty development programs. Prior to joining HCRC, Chantell served on the Mayor's Economic Development Staff in Brookfield Wisconsin, where she conducted research on federal and state legislation issues. Prior to that, Chantell conducted research for the Urban Research Center at the University of Wisconsin—Milwaukee, and for U.S. Senator Russ Feingold's Office. Chantell received her Master's in Public Administration from the University of Wisconsin—Milwaukee and her Bachelor's Degree in Political Science from the University of Wisconsin—Madison.

Brian J. Zucker, president and founder of Human Capital Research Corporation has seventeen years experience as an economist and policy analyst. Mr. Zucker has conducted more than 200 institution, state, and federal level higher education and economic development studies. A specialist in higher education finance and performance measurement, Mr. Zucker is frequently called upon to consult with and advise legislators, discuss his ideas about higher education with the press, and to utilize his creative approach to educational research in partnership with peer consultants. Mr. Zucker received his M.A. in Regional Science from the University of Pennsylvania and his B.A. in Anthropology from the University of Wisconsin—Madison.

Thomas A. Flint, Vice President for Lifelong Learning at CAEL has extensive experience in higher education. His work includes credit and non-credit instruction, committee work on the institutional functions of curriculum, accreditation, and admissions, and chairmanship of college committees on student outcomes assessment and new program development. With over 20 years' expertise in student financial aid management, Dr. Flint's name is recognized nationally among a variety of educators and policy analysts. His peer-reviewed research has been presented at ASHE, AIR, NACAC, and NASFAA national conferences, and he is a three-time recipient of NASFAA's sponsored research grants. He served on the project team of the College Board and NASFAA for their 1996 national study of undergraduate financial aid policies and on the technical review panel for the 1996 National Postsecondary Student Aid Study conducted by the Research Triangle Institute and U.S. Department of Education. Dr. Flint's numerous publications include scholarly articles for the *Journal of Higher Education, Research in Higher Education, Journal of College Admission,* and *Journal of Student Financial Aid.* Dr. Flint received his B.S. in Public Address and Group Communication from Northwestern University, his M.A. in Psychology from Roosevelt University, and his Ph.D. in Education, Curriculum and Instruction, from the University of Illinois at Chicago.

also from ouncil for dult and xperiential earning

Assessing Learning: A CAEL Handbook

by Susan Simosko provides the tools by which college faculty and administrators can develop skills and procedures for assessing adults' prior learning. It covers a wide range of topics—from the history and philosophy of experiential learning to the development of current assessment practices.

1988/179 pages/perfect/$17.50*/ISBN: 0-7872-3347-1

Assessing Learning: Standards, Principles, and Procedures

by Urban Whitaker builds on **Assessing Learning: A CAEL Handbook** by outlining the principles of good practice and standards of excellence in the assessment of learning. Assessment practitioners have welcomed this best-selling guide to evaluating learning.

1989/181 pages/perfect/$7.95*/ISBN: 0-7872-3346-3

Best Practices of College Business and Industry Centers: A Self-Improvement Guide

by Ruth Barber and Rebecca Klein-Collins is a comprehensive guide to peak performance for college business and industry centers. It provides a self-assessment tool for evaluating the practices and performance of any center.

1998/76 pages/3 hole drilled/$79.95*/ISBN: 0-7872-5579-3

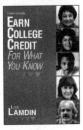

Earn College Credit for What You Know

by Lois Lamdin is written for adults who are considering returning to school. This guide encourages these adults to think about what they have learned in life, whether some of that learning may be appropriate for assessment for college credit, and exactly how to go about earning that credit.

1997/256 pages/perfect/$24.95*/ISBN: 0-7872-3573-3

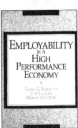

Employability in a High Performance Economy

by Barry Sheckley, Lois Lamdin, and Morris T. Keeton discusses the need for a more productive, better qualified workforce in order to maintain the long-term health and prosperity of the American economy. This important book spells out each essential component and objective of employability.

1993/236 pages/casebound/$29.95*/ISBN: 0-7872-3353-6

Higher Education and the Real World: The Story of CAEL

by Zelda F. Gamson details this success story in American education. From its founding in 1974 as a project of the Educational Testing Service to the present, CAEL has thrived when many other innovative organizations have had to cut back. Read this book and learn why!

1989/159 pages/casebound/$25.00*/ISBN: 0-7872-3358-7
1989/159 pages/perfect/$14.95*/ISBN: 0-7872-3359-8

Perspectives on Experiential Learning

edited by Morris T. Keeton was designed to help overcome some of the barriers that develop due to the different national and organizational perspectives people bring to experiential learning. This book helps establish a common frame of reference for discussion of the issues related to experience and learning.

1994/176 pages/perfect/$12.50*/ISBN: 0-7872-3352-8

Portfolio Development and Adult Learning

by Alan Mandell and Elana Michelson explores the eight approaches to portfolio development courses most typically used at colleges and universities, providing examples of each through a closer examination of prior learning assessment programs offered at 11 institutions of higher learning.

1990/174 pages/perfect/$21.50*/ISBN: 0-7872-3360-9

Prior Learning Assessment: Results of a Survey

by Mary Fugate and Ruth Chapman uses the results of a 1991 CAEL survey to document the use and acceptance of various prior learning assessment methodologies in post-secondary institutions throughout the U.S. This book provides comprehensive information on PLA for a variety of audiences.

1992/152 pages/perfect/$19.95*/ISBN: 0-7872-3351-X

Prior Learning Assessment: A Guidebook to American Institutional Practices

by Brian J. Zucker, Chantell C. Johnson, and Thomas A. Flint reviews and digests the results of this updated PLA survey. It addresses the changes and expansion in the use of PLA methods across the country since the previous survey in 1991.

NEW!

1998/160 pages/perfect/$24.95*/0-7872-5589-0

Roads to the Learning Society

by Lois Lamdin is comprised of insights from twenty of the leading experts in adult and experiential learning. Issues addressed include: portfolio assessment; the relationship between experiential learning and adult development; and the need and basis for guidelines for workforce policy-making at the state and national levels.

1991/163 pages/casebound/$25.00*/ISBN: 0-7872-3349-8

Your Hidden Credentials

by Peter Smith is based on the fact that the average adult worker now changes jobs six times before retiring and learns valuable skills in each work situation. This book reveals the stages for identifying and appreciating personal learning, and using it as a springboard to greater lifelong satisfaction and knowledge.

1986/181 pages/perfect/$7.95*/ISBN 0-7872-3346-3

Prices are subject to change without notice.

To order today call 1-800-228-0810
or complete the order form on the next page!

Please send me these CAEL titles!

Call
1-800-228-0810 to order by phone
1-800-772-9165 to FAX your order

Visit our website: www.kendallhunt.com

Send to:
Kendall/Hunt Publishing Company
4050 Westmark Drive, P.O. Box 1840
Dubuque, Iowa 52004-1840

Qty	Title/ISBN	Price	Total
	Assessing Learning: A CAEL Handbook/0-7872-3347-1	$17.50*	
	Assessing Learning: Standards, Principles and Procedures/0-7872-3346-3	7.95*	
	Best Practices of College Business and Industry Centers/0-7872-5579-3	79.95*	
	Earn College Credit for What You Know/0-7872-3573-3	24.95*	
	Employability in a High Performance Economy/0-7872-3353-6	29.95*	
	Higher Education and the Real World (casebound)/0-7872-3358-7	25.00*	
	Higher Education and the Real World (perfect)/0-7872-3359-5	14.95*	
	Perspectives on Experiential Learning/0-7872-3352-8	12.50*	
	Portfolio Development and Adult Learning/0-7872-3360-9	21.50*	
	Prior Learning Assessment: Results of a Survey/0-7872-3351-X	19.95*	
	Prior Learning Assessment: A Guidebook to American Institutional Practices/0-7872-5589-0	24.95*	
	Roads to the Learning Society/0-7872-3349-8	25.00*	
	Your Hidden Credentials/0-7872-3346-3	7.95*	
	AL, AZ, CA, CO, FL, GA, IA, IL, IN, KY, LA, MA, MD, MI, MN, NJ NY, OH, PA, TN, TX, VA, WA, & WI orders, please add appropriate sales tax.		
	Add $5 shipping for the first book, and $.50 each for additional books.		
		TOTAL	

☐ Check or money order enclosed, payable to Kendall/Hunt.

☐ Charge my account: ☐ VISA ☐ MasterCard ☐ American Express

Account # _____ Exp. Date _____/_____

Signature _____

Name _____

Organization_____

Address _____

City _____ State _____ ZIP _____

Phone ( ) _____ E-mail _____

KENDALL/HUNT PUBLISHING COMPANY
4050 Westmark Drive   P.O. Box 1840   Dubuque, Iowa 52004-1840

Prices are subject to change without notice.
A/B-01   dkz   48966024

more from Council for Adult and Experiential Learning

Improving Employee Development: Perspectives from Research and Practice
by Morris Keeton and Barry Sheckley

Essential reading for human resources/training professionals, researchers, and professors, this collection of case studies determines the six key principles of adult learning to consider when designing, delivering, and assessing employee development programs.

....$19.50* (CAEL member price $15.50)

If You Build It, Will They Come?

One-Stop Career Centers are the new assessment and referral brokers for adult learning, workforce development and job placement nationwide. **If You Build It, Will They Come?** is a case study of the Commonwealth of Massachusetts' establishment of a network of one-stop career centers.

....$5.00* (plus $1.50 postage and handling per copy)

Extending Education and Training Policy to Adult Workers: Lessons from the CAEL Workforce Education Model
by Erin Flynn, Laura Winters, and Carolyn Mark

This report examines the barriers intrinsic to the current system of workforce education and training and analyzes the impact of one approach to organizing that system; an approach developed by CAEL. Jobs for the Future (JFF) and CAEL undertook this study to analyze the impact of participation on individuals and employers at three companies that have implemented the CAEL approach to workforce education.

....$5.00* (plus $1.50 postage and handling per copy)

Prices are subject to change without notice.

- -

To order: Call CAEL at 312-922-5909, or complete this form and send it to:
CAEL Publications, 243 S. Wabash Avenue, Suite 800, Chicago, IL 60604

Please send me: ☐ **Improving Employee Development**
☐ **If You Build It, Will They Come?**
☐ **Extending Education and Training Policy to Adult Workers**

☐ Check or money order enclosed (payable to CAEL)   ☐ Charge my: ☐ VISA   ☐ Mastercard

Account # _____   Exp. Date _____/_____

Signature _____

Name _____

Address _____

City _____ State _____ ZIP _____